# Praise for *The Hard Thing About Hard Things*

"His book takes readers through Mr. Horowitz's own fascinating career, while sharing examples and dispensing advice drawn from the careers of others. . . . The honesty is both refreshing and compelling, and readers will enjoy being taken through challenge after challenge alongside Mr. Horowitz."
—*Wall Street Journal*

"With a candid, even profanity-laced style that quotes everyone from Silicon Valley legend Bill Campbell to hip-hop star Nas, Horowitz writes about what it takes to manage people and lead organizations today. . . . Even the most seasoned managers will appreciate Horowitz's discussion of the emotional toll of high-power jobs and what he calls the CEO psychological meltdown."
—*Washington Post*

"This isn't your traditional, how-to founder advice. He tackles the real problems and challenges entrepreneurs face. . . . But where Horowitz separates himself is in his advice around how to control your own psychology and demons as a CEO and founder. These are real problems that every CEO and leader faces, as sometimes they are their own worst enemy. . . . My bet is that Horowitz's book becomes gospel for startups. His stories already have."
—*Tech Crunch*

"The most valuable book on startup management hands down."
—*Pando Daily*

"Horowitz tends to dispense management advice in a kind of one-two punch. First comes the self-deprecating quip about mismanagement and misery, delivered with a knowing grin and capped with a two-beat chuckle. But soon the smile will vanish, and he'll turn dead serious. His brow will furrow slightly, his eyes will widen and focus with an intensity that borders on scary, and he'll speak slowly, deliberately. It's almost as if you can't afford not to listen."
—*Fortune*

"There is more than enough substance in Mr. Horowitz's impressive tome to turn it into a leadership classic."
—*Economist*

# THE
## Building a
# HARD
## Business When
# THING
## There Are No
# ABOUT
## Easy Answers
# HARD
## BEN HOROWITZ
# THINGS

**HARPER**
BUSINESS

*An Imprint of* HarperCollins*Publishers*
www.harpercollins.com

THE HARD THING ABOUT HARD THINGS. Copyright ©2014 by Ben Horowitz.
All rights reserved. Printed in the United States of America. No part of this
book may be used or reproduced in any manner whatsoever without written
permission except in the case of brief quotations embodied in critical articles
and reviews. For information, address HarperCollins Publishers, 195 Broadway,
New York, NY 10007.

HarperCollins books may be purchased for educational, business, or
sales promotional use. For information, please e-mail the Special Markets
Department at SPsales@harpercollins.com.

An extension of this copyright page appears on pages 287–89.

FIRST EDITION

*Designed by Jaime Putorti*

Library of Congress Cataloging-in-Publication Data has been applied for.

ISBN 978-0-06-227320-8

17  18   OV/RRD   20  19  18  17  16  15  14

This is for Felicia, Sophia, Mariah, and the Boocher,
*mi familia*, for putting up with me when I was learning
all of this.

---

One hundred percent of my portion of the proceeds of this
book will go to help women in developing countries gain
basic civil rights via the American Jewish World Service.
They truly face the hard things.

# CONTENTS

# INTRODUCTION

"This the real world, homie, school finished
They done stole your dreams, you dunno who did it."
—KANYE WEST, "GORGEOUS"

Every time I read a management or self-help book, I find myself saying, "That's fine, but that wasn't really the hard thing about the situation." The hard thing isn't setting a big, hairy, audacious goal. The hard thing is laying people off when you miss the big goal. The hard thing isn't hiring great people. The hard thing is when those "great people" develop a sense of entitlement and start demanding unreasonable things. The hard thing isn't setting up an organizational chart. The hard thing is getting people to communicate within the organization that you just designed. The hard thing isn't dreaming big. The hard thing is waking up in the middle of the night in a cold sweat when the dream turns into a nightmare.

The problem with these books is that they attempt to provide a recipe for challenges that have no recipes. There's no recipe for really complicated, dynamic situations. There's no recipe for building a high-tech company; there's no recipe for leading a group of people out of trouble; there's no recipe for making a series of hit songs; there's no recipe for playing NFL quarterback; there's no recipe for running for president; and there's no recipe for motivating teams when your business has turned to crap. That's the hard thing about hard things—there is no formula for dealing with them.

Nonetheless, there are many bits of advice and experience that can help with the hard things.

I do not attempt to present a formula in this book. Instead, I present my story and the difficulties that I have faced. As an entrepreneur, a CEO, and now as a venture capitalist, I still find these lessons useful—especially as I work with a new generation of founder-CEOs. Building a company inevitably leads to tough times. I've been there; I've done that. Circumstances may differ, but the deeper patterns and the lessons keep resonating.

For the past several years, I've encapsulated these lessons in a series of blog posts that have been read by millions of people. Many of those have reached out to me wanting to know the backstory to the lessons. This book tells that backstory for the first time and includes the related lessons from the blog. I've also been inspired by many friends, advisers, and family members who have helped me throughout my career and also by hip-hop/rap music. Because hip-hop artists aspire to be both great and successful and see themselves as entrepreneurs, many of the themes—competing, making money, being misunderstood—provide insight into the hard things. I share my experiences in the hope of providing clues and inspiration for others who find themselves in the struggle to build something out of nothing.

# THE
# HARD THING
# ABOUT
# HARD THINGS

# CHAPTER 1

# FROM COMMUNIST TO VENTURE CAPITALIST

"This here is all about
My wife, my kids, the life that I live
Through the night, I was his, it was right, but I did
My ups, and downs, my slips, my falls
My trials and tribulations, my heart, my balls."

—DMX, "WHO WE BE"

The other day I threw a big barbecue at my house and invited a hundred of my closest friends. These types of gatherings aren't unusual. My brother-in-law, Cartheu, and I have been barbecuing for years, and my skills have earned me the nickname from my African American friends "the Jackie Robinson of Barbecue." I crossed the color line.

At this particular barbecue, the conversation turned to the great rapper Nas. My friend Tristan Walker, a young African American entrepreneur, commented proudly that Nas was from his home project, Queensbridge, New York—one of the largest public housing projects in the United States. My seventy-three-year-old Jewish father interjected, "I've been to Queensbridge." Convinced that there was no way that my old, white father had been to Queensbridge, Tristan said, "You must mean *Queens*. Queensbridge is actually a housing project in an extremely rough neighborhood." My father insisted: No, it was Queensbridge.

I pointed out to Tristan that my father grew up in Queens, so he couldn't possibly be confused. Then I asked, "Dad, what were you doing in Queensbridge?" He replied, "I was passing out communist literature when I was eleven years old. I remember it well, because my mother got very upset that the Communist Party sent me into the projects. She thought it was too dangerous for a little kid."

My grandparents were actually card-carrying Communists. As an active member in the Communist Party, my grandfather Phil Horowitz lost his job as a schoolteacher during the McCarthy era. My father was a red-diaper baby and grew up indoctrinated in the philosophy of the left. In 1968, he moved our family west to Berkeley, California, and became editor of the famed New Left magazine *Ramparts*.

As a result, I grew up in the city affectionately known by its inhabitants as the People's Republic of Berkeley. As a young child, I was incredibly shy and terrified of adults. When my mother dropped me off at nursery school for the first time, I began to cry. The teacher told my mother to just leave, while reassuring her that crying was common among nursery school children. But when Elissa Horowitz returned three hours later, she found me soaking wet and still crying. The teacher explained that I hadn't stopped, and now my clothes were drenched as a result. I got kicked out of nursery school that day. If my mother hadn't been the most patient person in the world, I might never have gone to school. When everybody around her recommended psychiatric treatment, she was patient, willing to wait until I got comfortable with the world, no matter how long it took.

When I was five years old, we moved from a one-bedroom house on Glen Avenue, which had become far too small for a six-person family, to a larger one on Bonita Avenue. Bonita was middle-class Berkeley, which means something a bit different from what one finds in most middle-class neighborhoods. The block was a collection of hippies, crazy people, lower-class people working hard to move up, and upper-class people taking enough drugs to move down. One day, one of my older brother Jonathan's friends, Roger (not his real name), was over at our house. Roger pointed to an African American kid down the block who was riding in a red wagon. Roger dared me: "Go down the street, tell that kid to give you his wagon, and if he says anything, spit in his face and call him a nigger."

A few things require clarification here. First, we were in Berkeley, so that was not common language. In fact, I had never heard the word *nigger* before and didn't know what it meant, though I guessed it wasn't a compliment. Second, Roger wasn't racist and he wasn't raised in a bad home. His father was a Berkeley professor and both his parents were some of the nicest people in the world, but we later found out that Roger suffered from schizophrenia, and his dark side wanted to see a fight.

Roger's command put me in a difficult situation. I was terrified of Roger. I thought that he would surely give me a severe beating if I didn't follow his instructions. On the other hand, I was terrified of asking for the wagon. Hell, I was terrified of everything. I was much too scared of Roger to stay where I was, so I began walking down the block toward the other kid. The distance was probably thirty yards, but it felt like thirty miles. When I finally got there, I could barely move. I did not know what to say, so I just opened my mouth and started talking. "Can I ride in your wagon?" is what came out. Joel Clark Jr. said, "Sure." When I turned to see what Roger would do, he was gone. Apparently, his light side had taken over and he'd moved on to something else. Joel and I went on to play all day that day, and we've been best friends ever since. Eighteen years later, he would be the best man at my wedding.

Until now, I've never told that story to anyone, but it shaped my life. It taught me that being scared didn't mean I was gutless. What I did *mattered* and would determine whether I would be a hero or a coward. I have often thought back on that day, realizing that if I'd done what Roger had told me to do, I would have never met my best friend.

That experience also taught me not to judge things by their surfaces. Until you make the effort to get to know someone or something, you don't know anything. There are no shortcuts to knowledge, especially knowledge gained from personal experience. Following conventional wisdom and relying on shortcuts can be worse than knowing nothing at all.

## TURN YOUR SHIT IN

Over the years, I worked hard to avoid being influenced by first impressions and blindly adhering to convention. Growing up in Berkeley as an excellent student in a town that frowned upon football as being too militaristic, I wasn't expected to join the Berkeley High School football team, but that's what I did. This was a big step for me. I had not played in any of the peewee football leagues, so it was my first exposure to the sport. Nonetheless, those earlier lessons in dealing with fear helped me tremendously. In high school football, being able to handle fear is 75 percent of the game.

I will never forget the first team meeting with head coach Chico Mendoza. Coach Mendoza was a tough old guy who had played college football at Texas Christian University, home of the mighty Horned Frogs. Coach Mendoza began his opening speech, "Some of you guys will come out here and you just won't be serious. You'll get here and start shooting the shit, talking shit, bullshittin', not doing shit, and just want to look good in your football shit. If you do that, then you know what? Turn your shit in." He went on to elaborate on what was unacceptable: "Come late to practice? Turn your shit in. Don't want to hit? Turn your shit in. Walk on the grass? Turn your shit in. Call me Chico? Turn your shit in."

It was the most intense, hilarious, poetic speech I'd ever heard. I loved it. I couldn't wait to get home and tell my mother. She was horrified, but I still loved it. In retrospect, it was my first lesson in leadership. Former secretary of state Colin Powell says that leadership is the ability to get someone to follow you even if only out of curiosity. I was certainly curious to see what Coach Mendoza would say next.

I was the only kid on the football team who was also on the highest academic track in math, so my teammates and I didn't see each other in many classes. As a result, I ended up moving in multiple social circles and hanging out with kids with very different outlooks on the world. It amazed me how a diverse perspective utterly changed the meaning of every significant event in the world. For instance, when Run-D.M.C.'s *Hard Times* album came out, with its relentless bass drum, it sent an earthquake through the football team, but not even a ripple through my calculus class. Ronald Reagan's Strategic Defense Initiative was considered an outrage among young scientists due to its questionable technical foundation, but those aspects went unnoticed at football practice.

Looking at the world through such different prisms helped me separate facts from perception. This ability would serve me incredibly well later when I became an entrepreneur and CEO. In particularly dire circumstances when the "facts" seemed to dictate a certain outcome, I learned to look for alternative narratives and explanations coming from radically different perspectives to inform my outlook. The simple existence of an alternate, plausible scenario is often all that's needed to keep hope alive among a worried workforce.

## BLIND DATE

In the summer of 1986, I had finished my sophomore year of college at Columbia University, and I was staying with my father, who was now living in Los Angeles. I had been set up on a blind date by my friend and high school football teammate Claude Shaw. Claude and I got ready for the double date with his girlfriend, Jackie Williams, and my date, Felicia Wiley, by preparing an elaborate dinner. We meticulously planned and cooked all day and had the entire meal, including four perfectly presented T-bone steaks, ready at 7 p.m.—date time. But there were no dates. An hour passed, but we didn't get too worked up. Jackie was known for her tardiness, so no worries. Then two hours passed, and Claude called for a status check. I listened in shock as I looked over the now-cold gourmet meal that we'd prepared. My date, Felicia, had decided that she was "too tired" to show up for the date. Wow. How obnoxious!

I told Claude to hand me the phone. I introduced myself: "Hi, this is Ben, your blind date."

Felicia: "I am sorry, but I am tired and it is late."

Me: "Well, it is late, because you are *late*."

Felicia: "I know, but I am just too tired to come over."

At this point I decided to appeal to her sense of empathy.

Me: "Well, I understand your predicament, but the time to communicate this message would have been before we spent all day cooking dinner. At this point, anything short of getting into your car and driving here immediately would be rude and leave a permanently poor impression."

If she was totally self-centered (as she appeared to be), my plea would have no effect, and I would be better off missing the date. On the other hand, if she didn't want to go out like that, then there might be something there.

Felicia: "Okay, I'll come over."

Ninety minutes later she arrived wearing white shorts and looking as pretty as can be. In all my focus and anticipation about the date, I had completely forgotten about the fistfight I'd been in the day before. During a pickup basketball game in the San Fernando Valley, a six-foot-two-inch, crew-cut-sporting, camouflage-pants-wearing, fraternity-boy-looking player threw the ball at my brother. Jonathan was a musician, had long hair, and probably weighed about 155 pounds at the time. On the other hand, I was used to football and fighting and was ready for action. I judged the situation on my first impression, and I rushed the frat boy. A scuffle ensued. I landed some good punches but caught a right hook under my left eye, leaving a bit of a mark. It's possible that my target player was simply mad about a hard foul rather than trying to bully my brother, but that's the price of not taking the time to understand. I will never know.

Whatever the case, when I opened the door to greet our dates, Felicia's award-winning green eyes immediately fixed on the welt under my eye. Her first impression (told to me years later): "This guy is a thug. Coming here was a big mistake."

Fortunately, neither of us relied on our first impressions. We have been happily married for nearly twenty-five years and have three wonderful children.

## SILICON VALLEY

During one summer in college, I got a job as an engineer at a company called Silicon Graphics (SGI). The experience blew my mind. The company invented modern computer graphics and powered a whole new class set of applications ranging from the movie *Terminator 2* to amazing flight simulators. Everybody there was so smart. The things they built were so cool. I wanted to work for Silicon Graphics for the rest of my life.

After graduating from college and graduate school in computer science, I went back to work for SGI. Being there was a dream come true and I loved it. After my first year at SGI, I met a former head of marketing for the company, Roselie Buonauro, who had a new startup. Roselie had heard about me from her daughter, who also worked with me at SGI. Roselie recruited me hard. Eventually, she got me and I went to work for her at NetLabs.

Joining NetLabs turned out to be a horrible decision for me. The company was run by Andre Schwager, a former Hewlett-Packard executive, and more important, Roselie's husband. Andre and Roselie had been brought in by the venture capitalists as the "professional management team." Unfortunately, they understood very little about the products or the technology, and they sent the company off in one crazy direction after the next. This was the first time that I started to understand the importance of founders running their companies.

To make matters more complicated, my second daughter, Mariah, had been diagnosed with autism, which made working at a startup a terrible burden for our family, as I needed to spend more time at home.

One very hot day my father came over for a visit. We could not afford air-conditioning, and all three children were crying as my father and I sat there sweating in the 105-degree heat.

My father turned to me and said, "Son, do you know what's cheap?"

Since I had absolutely no idea what he was talking about, I replied, "No, what?"

"Flowers. Flowers are really cheap. But do you know what's expensive?" he asked.

Again, I replied, "No, what?"

He said, "Divorce."

Something about that joke, which was not really a joke, made me realize that I had run out of time. Up until that point, I had not really made any serious choices. I felt like I had unlimited bandwidth and could do everything in life that I wanted to do simultaneously. But his joke made it suddenly clear that by continuing on the course I was on, I might lose my family. By doing everything, I would fail at the most important thing. It was the first time that I forced myself to look at the world through priorities that were not purely my own. I thought that I could pursue my career, all my interests, and build my family. More important, I always thought about myself first. When you are part of a family or part of a group, that kind of thinking can get you into trouble, and I was in deep trouble. In my mind, I was confident that I was a good person and not selfish, but my actions said otherwise. I had to stop being a boy and become a man. I had to put first things first. I had to consider the people who I cared about most before considering myself.

I decided to quit NetLabs the next day. I found a job at Lotus Development that would allow me to get my home life straightened out. I stopped thinking about myself and focused on what was best for my family. I started being the person that I wanted to be.

## NETSCAPE

One day while working at Lotus, one of my coworkers showed me a new product called Mosaic, which was developed by some students at the University of Illinois. Mosaic was essentially a graphical interface to the Internet—a technology formerly only used by scientists and researchers. It amazed me. It was so obviously the future, and I was so obviously wasting my time working on anything but the Internet.

Several months later, I read about a company called Netscape, which had been cofounded by former Silicon Graphics founder Jim Clark and Mosaic inventor Marc Andreessen. I instantly decided that I should interview for a job there. I called a friend who worked at Netscape and asked if he could get me an interview with the company. He obliged and I was on my way.

During the first interviews, I met everyone on the product management team. I thought the meetings went well, but when I arrived home that evening Felicia was in tears. The Netscape recruiter had called me to give me some tips, and Felicia had answered. (This was before the days of pervasive cell phones.) The recruiter informed her that it would be unlikely I'd get the job, because the group was looking for candidates with Stanford or Harvard MBAs. Felicia suggested that maybe I could go back to school. Given that we had three children, she knew this was unrealistic, hence the tears. I explained that recruiters were not hiring managers, and that they might consider me despite my lack of proper business schooling.

The next day the hiring manager called back to let me know that they wanted me to interview with cofounder and Chief Technical Officer Marc Andreessen. He was twenty-two years old at the time.

In retrospect, it's easy to think both the Web browser and the Internet were inevitable, but without Marc's work, it is likely that we would be living in a very different world. At the time most people believed only scientists and researchers would use the Internet. The Internet was thought to be too arcane, insecure, and slow to meet real business needs. Even after the introduction of Mosaic, the world's first browser, almost nobody thought the Internet would be significant beyond the scientific community—least of all the most important technology industry leaders, who were busy building proprietary alternatives. The overwhelming favorites to dominate the race to become the so-called Information Superhighway were competing proprietary technologies from industry powerhouses such as Oracle and Microsoft. Their stories captured the imagination of the business press. This was not so illogical, since most companies didn't even run TCP/IP (the software foundation for the Internet)—they ran proprietary networking protocols such as AppleTalk, NetBIOS, and SNA. As late as November 1995, Bill Gates wrote a book titled *The Road Ahead*, in which he predicted that the Information Superhighway—a network connecting all businesses and consumers in a world of frictionless commerce—would be the logical successor to the Internet and would rule the future. Gates later went back and changed references from the Information Superhighway to the Internet, but that was not his original vision.

The implications of this proprietary vision were not good for business or for consumers. In the minds of visionaries like Bill Gates and Larry Ellison, the corporations that owned the Information Superhighway would tax every transaction by charging a "vigorish," as Microsoft's then–chief technology officer, Nathan Myhrvold, referred to it.

It's difficult to overstate the momentum that the proprietary Information Superhighway carried. After Mosaic, even Marc and his cofounder, Jim Clark, originally planned a business for video distribution to run on top of the proprietary Information Superhighway, not the Internet. It wasn't until deep into the planning process that they decided that by improving the browser to make it secure, more functional, and easier to use, they could make the Internet the network of the future. And that became the mission of Netscape—a mission that they would gloriously accomplish.

Interviewing with Marc was like no other job interview I'd ever had. Gone were questions about my résumé, my career progression, and my work habits. He replaced them with a dizzying inquiry into the history of email, collaboration software, and what the future might hold. I was an expert in the topic, because I'd spent the last several years working on the leading products in the category, but I was shocked by how much a twenty-two-year-old kid knew about the history of the computer business. I'd met many really smart young people in my career, but never a young technology historian. Marc's intellect and instincts took me aback, but beyond Marc's historical knowledge, his insights about technologies such as replication were incisive and on point. After the interview, I phoned my brother and told him that I'd just interviewed with Marc Andreessen, and I thought that he might be the smartest person I'd ever met.

A week later, I got the job. I was thrilled. I didn't really care what the offer was. I knew that Marc and Netscape would change the world, and I wanted to be part of it. I could not wait to get started.

Once at Netscape, I was put in charge of their Enterprise Web Server product line. The line consisted of two products: the regular Web server, which listed for $1,200, and the secure Web server (a Web server that included the then brand-new security protocol invented by Netscape called SSL, Secure Sockets Layer) for $5,000. At the time that I joined, we had two engineers working on the Web servers: Rob McCool, who had invented the NCSA Web server, and his twin brother, Mike McCool.

By the time Netscape went public in August 1995, we had grown the Web server team to about nine engineers. The Netscape initial public offering (IPO) was both spectacular and historic. The stock initially priced at $14 per share, but a last-minute decision doubled the initial offering to $28 per share. It spiked to $75—nearly a record for a first-day gain—and closed at $58, giving Netscape a market value of nearly $3 billion on the day of the IPO. More than that, the IPO was an earthquake in the business world. As my friend and investment banker Frank Quattrone said at the time, "No one wanted to tell their grandchildren that they missed out on this one."

The deal changed everything. Microsoft had been in business for more than a decade before its IPO; we'd been alive for sixteen months. Companies began to get defined as "new economy" or as "old economy." And the new economy was winning. The *New York Times* called the Netscape IPO "world-shaking."

But there was a crack in our armor: Microsoft announced that it would be bundling its browser, Internet Explorer, with its upcoming breakthrough operating system release, Windows 95—for free. This posed a huge problem to Netscape, because nearly all of our revenue came from browser sales, and Microsoft controlled more than 90 percent of operating systems. Our answer to investors: We would make our money on Web servers.

Two months later, we got our hands on an early release of Microsoft's upcoming Web server Internet Information Server (IIS). We deconstructed IIS and found that it had every feature that we had—including the security in our high-end product—and was five times faster. Uh-oh. I figured that we had about five months before Microsoft released IIS to solve the problem or else we would be toast. In the "old economy," product cycles typically took eighteen months to complete, so this was an exceptionally short time frame even in the "new economy." So I went to see our department head, Mike Homer.

With the possible exception of Marc, Mike Homer was the most significant creative force behind Netscape. More important, the worse a situation became, the stronger Mike would get. During particularly brutal competitive attacks, most executives would run from the press. Mike, on the other hand, was always front and center. When Microsoft unveiled its famous "embrace and extend" strategy—a dramatic pivot to attack Netscape—Mike took every phone call, sometimes even talking to two reporters at once with a phone in each hand. He was the ultimate warrior.

Mike and I spent the next several months developing a comprehensive answer to Microsoft's threat. If they were going to give our products away, then we were going to offer a dirt-cheap, open alternative to the highly expensive and proprietary Microsoft BackOffice product line. To do so, we acquired two companies, which provided us with a competitive alternative to Microsoft Exchange. We then cut a landmark deal with the database company Informix to provide us unlimited relational database access through the Web for $50 a copy, which was literally hundreds of times less than Microsoft charged. Once we assembled the entire package, Mike named it Netscape SuiteSpot, as it would be the "suite" that displaced Microsoft's Back-Office. We lined everything up for a major launch on March 5, 1996, in New York.

Then, just two weeks before the launch, Marc, without telling Mike or me, revealed the entire strategy to the publication *Computer Reseller News*. I was livid. I immediately sent him a short email:

> To: Marc Andreessen
> Cc: Mike Homer
> From: Ben Horowitz
> Subject : Launch
> I guess we're not going to wait until the 5th to launch the strategy.
> —Ben

Within fifteen minutes, I received the following reply.

To: Ben Horowitz

Cc: Mike Homer, Jim Barksdale (CEO), Jim Clark (Chairman)

From: Marc Andreessen

Subject: Re: Launch

Apparently you do not understand how serious the situation is. We are getting killed killed killed out there. Our current product is radically worse than the competition. We've had nothing to say for months. As a result, we've lost over $3B in market capitalization. We are now in danger of losing the entire company and it's all server product management's fault.

Next time do the fucking interview yourself.

Fuck you,

Marc

I received this email the same day that Marc appeared barefoot and sitting on a throne on the cover of *Time* magazine. When I first saw the cover, I felt thrilled. I had never met anyone in my life who had been on the cover of *Time*. Then I felt sick. I brought both the magazine and the email home to Felicia to get a second opinion. I was very worried. I was twenty-nine years old, had a wife and three children, and needed my job. She looked at the email and the magazine cover and said, "You need to start looking for a job right away."

In the end, I didn't get fired and over the next two years, SuiteSpot grew from nothing to a $400 million a year business. More shocking, Marc and I eventually became friends; we've been friends and business partners ever since.

People often ask me how we've managed to work effectively across three companies over eighteen years. Most business relationships either become too tense to tolerate or not tense enough to be productive after a while. Either people challenge each other to the point where they don't like each other or they become complacent about each other's feedback and no longer benefit from the relationship. With Marc and me, even after eighteen years, he upsets me almost every day by finding something wrong in my thinking, and I do the same for him. It works.

## STARTING A COMPANY

At the end of 1998 and under immense pressure from Microsoft, which used the full force of its operating system monopoly to subsidize free products in every category in which Netscape competed, we sold the company to America Online (AOL). In the short term, this was a big victory for Microsoft since it had driven its biggest threat into the arms of a far less threatening competitor. In the long term, however, Netscape inflicted irreparable damage on Microsoft's stronghold on the computing industry: our work moved developers from Win32 API, Microsoft's proprietary platform, to the Internet. Someone writing new functionality for computers no longer wrote for Microsoft's proprietary platform. Instead, they wrote to the Internet and World Wide Web's standard interfaces. Once Microsoft lost its grip on developers, it became only a matter of time before it lost its monopoly on operating systems. Along the way, Netscape invented many of the foundational technologies of the modern Internet, including Java-Script, SSL, and cookies.

Once inside AOL, I was assigned to run the e-commerce platform and Marc became the chief technology officer. After a few months, it became apparent to both of us that AOL saw itself as more of a media company than a technology company. Technology enabled great new media projects, but the strategy was a media strategy and the top executive, Bob Pittman, was a genius media executive. Media companies focused on things like creating great stories whereas technology companies focused on creating a better way of doing things. We began to think about new ideas and about forming a new company.

In the process, we added two other potential cofounders to the discussion. Dr. Timothy Howes was coinventor of the Lightweight

Directory Access Protocol (LDAP), a masterful simplification of its byzantine X.500 predecessor. We hired Tim into Netscape in 1996 and together we successfully made LDAP the Internet directory standard. To this day, if a program is interested in information about a person, it accesses that information via LDAP. The fourth member of our team was In Sik Rhee, who had cofounded an application server company called Kiva Systems, which Netscape had acquired. He had been acting as CTO of the e-commerce division that I ran and, in particular, worked closely with the partner companies in making sure that they could handle the AOL scale.

As we discussed ideas, In Sik complained that every time we tried to connect an AOL partner on the AOL e-commerce platform, the partner's site would crash, because it couldn't handle the traffic load. Deploying software to scale to millions of users was totally different from making it work for thousands. And it was extremely complicated.

Hmm, there ought to be a company that does all that for them.

As we expanded the idea, we landed on the concept of a computing cloud. The term *cloud* had been used previously in the telecommunications industry to describe the smart cloud that handled all the complexity of routing, billing, and the like, so that one could plug a dumb device into the smart cloud and get all the smart functionality for free. We thought the same concept was needed in computing, so that software developers wouldn't have to worry about security, scaling, and disaster recovery. And if you are going to build a cloud, it should be big and loud, and that's how Loudcloud was born. Interestingly, the most lasting remnant of Loudcloud is the name itself, as the word *cloud* hadn't been previously used to describe a computing platform.

We incorporated the company and set out to raise money. It was 1999.

# CHAPTER 2

# "I WILL SURVIVE"

"Did you think I'd crumble?
Did you think I'd lay down and die?
Oh no, not I
I will survive."

—GLORIA GAYNOR, "I WILL SURVIVE"

**C**oming off the success of Netscape, Marc knew all the top venture capitalists in Silicon Valley, so we needed no introductions. Unfortunately for us, Kleiner Perkins, the firm that backed Netscape, had already funded a potentially competitive company. We spoke to all the other top-tier firms and decided to go with Andy Rachleff of Benchmark Capital.

If I had to describe Andy with one word, it would be *gentleman*. Smart, refined, and gracious, Andy was a brilliant abstract thinker who could encapsulate complex strategies into pithy sentences with ease. Benchmark would invest $15 million at a pre-money valuation (the value of the company before the cash goes into the company treasury) of $45 million. In addition, Marc would invest $6 million, bringing the total value of the company including its cash to $66 million, and would serve as our "full-time chairman of the board." Tim Howes would be our chief technology officer. I would be CEO. Loudcloud was two months old.

The valuation and the size of the funding were signs of the times and created an imperative to get big and capture the market before similarly well-funded competitors could. Andy said to me, "Ben, think about how you might run the business if capital were free."

Two months later, we would raise an additional $45 million from Morgan Stanley in debt with no covenants and no payments for three years, so Andy's question was more reality-based than you might think. Nonetheless, "What would you do if capital were free?" is a dangerous question to ask an entrepreneur. It's kind of like asking a fat person, "What would you do if ice cream had the exact same nutritional value as broccoli?" The thinking this question leads to can be extremely dangerous.

Naturally, I took the advice and ran with it. We quickly built out our cloud infrastructure and began signing up customers at a rapid rate. Within seven months of founding, we'd already booked $10 million in contracts. Loudcloud was taking off, but we were in a race against time and the competition. This meant hiring the best people and fielding the broadest cloud service, and that meant spending money—lots of it.

Our ninth hire was a recruiter, and we hired a human resources person when we had a dozen employees. We were hiring thirty employees a month and snagging many of the Valley's smartest people. One of our new recruits had quit his job at AOL to spend two months mountain climbing, but instead he joined us; another forfeited millions to join Loudcloud when he resigned from another company on the day of its IPO. Six months in, we had nearly two hundred employees.

Silicon Valley was on fire, and Loudcloud was billed in a *Wired* cover story as "Marc Andreessen's second coming." We traded our first office—where you'd blow a circuit if you ran the microwave and coffeemaker at the same time—for a fifteen-thousand-square-foot warehouse in Sunnyvale, which was too small for us by the time we moved in.

We spent $5 million to move into a new three-story stucco building with jade-colored tiles we called "the Taj" (as in the Taj Mahal). It was also too small to keep pace with our hiring frenzy, and people were sitting in the hallways. We rented a third parking lot down the street and ran shuttle vans to the office. (The neighbors hated us.) The kitchen was stocked like Costco, and when we fired the snack contractor for making our fridge look like the one in Philip Roth's *Goodbye, Columbus*, he asked for equity.

This was the time.

In the next quarter, we booked $27 million worth of new contracts, and we were less than nine months old. It seemed like we were building the greatest business of all time. Then came the great dot-com crash. The NASDAQ peaked at 5,048.62 on March 10, 2000—more than double its value from the year before—and then fell by 10 percent ten days later. A *Barron's* cover story titled "Burning Up" predicted what was to come. By April, after the government declared Microsoft a monopoly, the index plummeted even further. Startups lost massive value, investors lost massive wealth, and dot-coms, once heralded as the harbinger of a new economy, went out of business almost overnight and became known as dot-bombs. The NASDAQ eventually fell below 1,200, an 80 percent drop from its peak.

We thought our business might have been the fastest growing of all time at that point. That was the good news. The bad news was that we needed to raise even more money in this disastrous climate; nearly all of the $66 million in equity and debt we had raised had already been deployed in our quest to build the number-one cloud service and to support our now fast-growing set of customers.

The dot-com crash had spooked investors, so raising money wasn't going to be easy, especially since most of our customers were dot-com startups. This became quite clear when we pitched the deal to the Japanese firm Softbank Capital. My friend and Loudcloud board member Bill Campbell knew the Softbank people well and offered to get some "back-channel" information following the pitch. When my assistant told me that Bill was on the line, I quickly answered the phone. I was eager to hear where we stood.

I asked, "Bill, what did they say?" Bill replied in his raspy, coach's voice, "Ben, well, honestly, they thought you were smoking crack." With nearly three hundred employees and very little cash left, I felt like I was going to die. It was the first time I'd felt that way as CEO of Loudcloud, but not nearly the last.

During this time I learned the most important rule of raising money privately: Look for a market of one. You only need one investor to say yes, so it's best to ignore the other thirty who say "no." We eventually found investors for a series C round (meaning our third round of funding) at an amazing $700 million pre-money valuation and raised $120 million. The sales forecast for the quarter came in at $100 million, and things seemed like they might be okay. I felt confident that our sales forecasts would hold up given that previous forecasts had underestimated actual performance. And perhaps, I speculated, we could seamlessly migrate our customer base away from dot-com bombs to more stable, traditional customers such as Nike, our largest customer at the time.

And then the wheels came off.

We finished the third quarter of 2000 with $37 million in bookings—not the $100 million that we had forecast. The dot-com implosion turned out to be far more catastrophic than we had predicted.

## EUPHORIA AND TERROR

I needed to raise money yet again. Only this time the environment was even worse. In the fourth quarter of 2000, I met with every possible funding source, including Prince Al-Waleed bin Talal of Saudi Arabia, but nobody was willing to invest money at any valuation. We'd gone from being the hottest startup in Silicon Valley to unfundable in six months. With 477 employees and a business that resembled a ticking time bomb, I searched for answers.

Thinking about what might happen if we ran completely out of money—laying off all the employees that I'd so carefully selected and hired, losing all my investors' money, jeopardizing all the customers who trusted us with their business—made it difficult to concentrate on the possibilities. Marc Andreessen attempted to cheer me up with a not-so-funny-at-the-time joke:

Marc: "Do you know the best thing about startups?"

Ben: "What?"

Marc: "You only ever experience two emotions: euphoria and terror. And I find that lack of sleep enhances them both."

With the clock ticking, one unattractive but intriguing option emerged: We could go public. In an oddity of the times, the private funding market shut down for companies with our profile, but the window on the public market remained just slightly open. This may sound like a crazy anomaly and it was, but private funds had become completely cynical while the public markets were only 80 percent of the way there.

With no other options available, I needed to propose to the board that we go public. In order to prepare, I made a list of the pros and cons of an IPO.

I knew that Bill Campbell would be the critical person I'd need to persuade one way or another. Bill was the only one of our board members who had been a public company CEO. He knew the pros and cons better than anyone else. More important, everybody always seemed to defer to Bill in these kinds of sticky situations, because Bill had a special quality about him.

At the time, Bill was in his sixties, with gray hair and a gruff voice, yet he had the energy of a twenty-year-old. He began his career as a college football coach and did not enter the business world until he was forty. Despite the late start, Bill eventually became the chairman and CEO of Intuit. Following that, he became a legend in high tech, mentoring great CEOs such as Steve Jobs of Apple, Jeff Bezos of Amazon, and Eric Schmidt of Google.

Bill is extremely smart, super-charismatic, and elite operationally, but the key to his success goes beyond those attributes. In any situation—whether it's the board of Apple, where he's served for over a decade; the Columbia University Board of Trustees, where he is chairman; or the girls' football team that he coaches—Bill is inevitably everybody's favorite person.

People offer many complex reasons for why Bill rates so highly. In my experience it's pretty simple. No matter who you are, you need two kinds of friends in your life. The first kind is one you can call when something good happens, and you need someone who will be excited for you. Not a fake excitement veiling envy, but a real excitement. You need someone who will actually be more excited for you than he would be if it had happened to him. The second kind of friend is somebody you can call when things go horribly wrong—when your life is on the line and you only have one phone call. Who is it going to be? Bill Campbell is both of those friends.

I presented my thinking as follows: "We have not been able to find any investors in the private markets. Our choices are to either keep working on private funding or start preparing to go public. While our prospects for raising money privately seem quite difficult, going public has a large number of issues:

- "Our sales processes are not robust and it's difficult to forecast in any environment.

- "We are not in any environment; we are in a rapidly declining environment and it's not clear where the bottom is.

- "Our customers are going bankrupt at an alarming and unpredictable rate.

- "We are losing money and will be losing money for quite some time.

- "We are not operationally sound.

- "In general, we are not ready to be public."

The board listened carefully. Their expressions showed deep concern with the issues I'd raised and an awkwardly long silence ensued. As expected, Bill broke the dead air.

"Ben, it's not the money."

I felt a strange sense of relief. Maybe we didn't have to go public. Maybe I'd overestimated our cash problems. Perhaps there was another way.

Then Bill spoke again, "It's the *fucking* money."

Okay, I guess we're going public.

In addition to the issues I had outlined for the board, our business was complex and hard for investors to understand. We typically signed customers to two-year contracts, and then recognized the revenue monthly. This model is now common, but it was quite unusual then. Given the fast growth in our bookings, revenue lagged behind new bookings by quite a bit. As a result, our S-1 (our registration with the SEC) stated that we had $1.94 million in trailing six months revenue, and we forecast $75 million for the following year—an incredibly steep revenue ramp. Since earnings are driven by revenue and not bookings, we had gigantic losses. In addition, the stock option rules at the time made it seem like our losses were about four times as large as they actually were. These factors led to extremely negative press heading into the IPO.

A scathing story in *Red Herring*, for instance, noted that our list of customers was "quite thin" and that we were too reliant on dot-coms. It quoted a Yankee Group analyst positing that we had "lost something like $1 million dollars per employee over the last 12 months," and conjecturing that the way we did it was by having a bonfire in the parking lot and getting everyone busy burning dollar bills. *Business-Week* took us apart in an article that declared us "the IPO from hell." A *Wall Street Journal* cover piece quoted a money manager's reaction to our offering as "Wow, they were desperate." One financier—who actually invested in the offering—called it "the best option among a particularly ugly set of options."

Despite the horrifying press, we prepared to hit the road. Benchmarking ourselves against comparable companies, we settled on the price of the offering at $10 per share after an upcoming reverse split, which would value the company at just under $700 million—less than the valuation from the previous private round of financing, but much better than bankruptcy.

It was not at all clear that we would be successful with the offering. The stock market was crashing, and the public market investors we visited were visibly distressed.

At the end of the preparation process and after the banks had signed off, our director of finance, Scott Kupor, received a call from our banker at Morgan Stanley.

Banker: "Scott, did you know that $27.6 million of your cash is restricted and tied up in real estate commitments?"

Scott: "Yes, of course."

Banker: "So, you have just over three weeks' worth of cash before you go bankrupt?"

Scott: "Yes."

Scott then relayed the conversation to me, saying, "Can you believe they underwrote the deal and didn't notice that the cash was restricted until now? We gave them all the documents."

Right before we were to leave for the IPO road show, I called an all-company meeting to share two pieces of news: First, we were going public, or at least we were going to try to go public. Second, the company had fallen so far in value that we would have to reverse split the stock two for one.

I thought the first part would go okay, but I was worried about how the second piece of news would be received. We had to reverse split the stock to get the price per share high enough to go public. In theory, a reverse split shouldn't matter at all. Each employee owned a certain percentage of the company. The company had a total number of shares of stock. Multiply the total number of shares by the percentage, and you get the employees' share number. Cut the number of shares in half and, while employees would have half the number of shares, they'd still own the exact same percentage of the company. Nothing changed.

Oh, but it did. As we grew from zero to six hundred employees in less than eighteen months, the stage was set for hyperbole and momentum. Some overly excited managers oversold the dream. They spoke only in terms of shares rather than in percentages and spun stories of a potential $100 per share stock price. Employees then calculated their fantasy price per share and figured out how much money they would make. I was aware that this was going on, but I never thought we would reverse split the stock, so I never worried about it. Like many other things that I screwed up during that period, I should have worried.

My wife, Felicia, came to the all-company meeting as she always did. This time her parents were in town, so they came, too. The meeting did not go well. People did not realize how close to the edge we were, so the news of the IPO didn't make anyone happy. The news of the reverse split made them even less happy—in fact, it infuriated them. I had literally cut their fantasy number in half, and they were not pleased about it. Nobody said harsh things directly to me. My in-laws, however, heard everything. And, as my father-in-law put it, "it wasn't nothin' nice."

My mother-in-law, Loretta, asked my wife, "Why does everybody hate Ben so much?" Felicia, who is normally the most electric, outgoing person in any room, was just recovering from hernia surgery so she wasn't her normal bubbly self. She was discouraged. My in-laws were depressed. The employees were pissed. I had no idea if I'd be able to raise the money. What a way to start a road show, an event that's usually the cause of a bit more fanfare.

The road show was brutal. The stock market crashed daily, and technology stocks were to blame. Investors looked like they'd come out of torture chambers when we arrived. One mutual fund manager looked right at Marc and me and asked, "Why are you here? Do you have any idea what's going on in the world?" I thought that there was no way we'd be able to raise the money. We were going to go bankrupt for sure. I did not sleep more than two hours total during that entire three-week trip.

Three days into the tour, I received a call from my father-in-law. John Wiley had been through a lot in his seventy-one years. As a boy, his father was murdered in Texas. In order to survive, he and his mother moved in with an unkind man and his nine children. There, John was abused, made to stay in the barn with the animals, while the other children ate his dinner. Eventually, John and his mother left that cruelty by walking for three days down a dirt road, carrying everything they owned. John would recall that journey in great detail his entire life. As a young man, before finishing his high school education, he left home to fight in the Korean War so that he could support his mother. As a young father of five, he took every job imaginable to support his family, including unloading banana boats and working to build the Alaskan pipeline. He tragically saw two of his children die before he reached the age of sixty. He had a hard life and was used to bad news.

John Wiley did not call me for casual reasons. If he called, it was serious, possibly even deadly serious.

Ben: "Hello."

John: "Ben, the office said not to bother you, but I just want to let you know that Felicia stopped breathing, but she is not going to die."

Ben: "Not going to die? What?!?! What happened?"

I could not believe it. I had been so focused on work that I had lost focus of the only thing that really mattered to me. Once again, I neglected to worry about the one thing that I should have worried about.

Ben: "What happened?"

John: "They gave her some medicine and she had an allergic reaction and she stopped breathing, but she's okay now."

Ben: "When?"

John: "Yesterday."

Ben: "What? Why didn't you tell me?"

John: "I knew that you were busy and that you were really in trouble at work because of that meeting that I went to."

Ben: "Should I come home?"

John: "Oh no. We'll take care of her. You just take care of what you need to do."

I was completely stunned. I started sweating so hard that I had to change my clothes right after the call. I had no idea what to do. If I returned home, the company would surely go bankrupt. If I stayed . . . how could I stay? I called back and had him put Felicia on the phone.

Ben: "If you need me, I will come home."

Felicia: "No. Get the IPO done. There is no tomorrow for you and the company. I'll be fine."

I stumbled through the rest of the road show completely discombobulated. One day I wore a mismatching suit jacket and suit pants, which Marc pointed out to me midway through the meeting. I had no idea where I was half the time. During the three weeks we were on the road, comparable companies in our market lost half of their value, which meant that our $10 share price was roughly double the current benchmark. The bankers recommended that we lower the price of the offering to $6 a share in order to reflect this new reality, but they gave us no assurance that the deal would actually get done. Then, the day before the offering, Yahoo, the lighthouse company of the Internet boom, announced Tim Koogle, its CEO, was stepping down. We had hit the nadir of the dot-com crash.

The Loudcloud offering finally sold at $6 a share, and we raised $162.5 million, but there was no celebration and no party. Neither Goldman Sachs nor Morgan Stanley—the two banks that took us public—even offered us the traditional closing dinner. It may have been the least celebratory IPO in history. But Felicia was feeling better, and we had pulled it off. In a brief moment of lightheartedness on the plane ride home, I turned to Scott Kupor, my director of finance, and said, "We did it!" He replied, "Yeah, but we're still fucked."

Years later, in 2012, after Yahoo fired its CEO, Scott Thompson, Felicia mused, "Should they bring back Koogle?" I replied, "Tim Koogle? How do you even know who Tim Koogle is?" She then relived the conversation we'd had eleven years earlier. It went something like this:

Ben: "We're fucked."

Felicia: "What do you mean? What happened?"

Ben: "Yahoo fired Koogle. It's over. The whole thing is over."

Felicia: "Who is Koogle?"

Ben: "He was the CEO of Yahoo. We're fucked. I'm going to have to shut the company down."

Felicia: "Are you sure?"

Ben: "Didn't you hear me? They fired Koogle. We're fucked."

She had never seen me that depressed before, and she never forgot it. For most CEOs, the night before their public offering is a highlight. For me, it was a highlight of depression.

## IF YOU ARE GOING TO EAT SHIT,
## DON'T NIBBLE

During the road show, as a way to break the tension, Marc would say, "Remember, Ben, things are always darkest before they go completely black." He was joking, but as we entered our first quarter as a public company, those words seemed prescient. Customers continued to churn, the macroeconomic environment worsened, and our sales prospects declined. As we got closer to our first earnings call with investors, I conducted a thorough review to make sure that we were still on track to meet our guidance.

The good news was that we would meet our forecast for the quarter. The bad news: There was very little chance that we would meet our forecast for the year. Typically, investors expect that companies will refrain from going public if they can't hit at least their first year's forecast. These were exceptional times, but resetting guidance on your very first earnings call was still a very bad thing to do.

As we discussed where to reset guidance to investors, we were faced with a tough choice: Should we try to minimize the initial damage by taking down the number as little as possible or should we minimize the risk of another reset? If we reduced the number by a lot, the stock might fall apart. On the other hand, if we didn't lower it enough, we might have to reset again, which would cost us all the credibility we had left. My controller, Dave Conte, raised his hand with what would be the definitive advice: "No matter what we say, we're going to get killed. As soon as we reset guidance, we'll have no credibility with investors, so we might as well take all the pain now, because nobody will believe any positivity in the forecast anyway. If you are going to eat shit, don't nibble." So we reset guidance for the year, slashing our original forecast of $75 million in projected revenue to $55 million.

Resetting revenue guidance also meant resetting expense guidance, and that meant laying people off. We'd been the darling of the startup world, and now I had to send home 15 percent of our employees. It was the clearest indication yet that I was failing. Failing my investors, failing my employees, and failing myself.

Following the reset, Goldman Sachs and Morgan Stanley—the investment banks that had taken us public—both dropped research coverage, meaning their analysts would no longer follow the company's progress on behalf of their clients. This was a huge slap in the face and a massive reneging of the promises they made when they were pitching us, but times were tough all around, and we had no recourse. With a vote of no confidence from our banks and a lowered revenue forecast, the stock price plummeted from $6 a share to $2.

Despite the mammoth negative momentum, we soldiered on, and were putting together a fairly strong quarter in the third quarter of

2001. Then, on September 11, terrorists hijacked four jetliners, flying two into the World Trade Center and another into the Pentagon, and in the end throwing the whole world into chaos. It turned out that our largest deal that quarter was with the British government. It represented one-third of our bookings, and we would miss the quarter's targets badly without it. Our champion on the deal called to inform us that Prime Minister Tony Blair had redirected the funds for our deal to the war chest—literally. By some miracle our sales director convinced one of Tony Blair's staffers to get the money back, so we got the deal and made the quarter.

Nonetheless, the close call was a sign to me that the entire operation was far too fragile. I got another sign when our largest competitor, Exodus, filed for bankruptcy on September 26. It was a truly incredible bankruptcy in that the company had been valued at $50 billion a little more than a year earlier. It was also remarkable because Exodus had raised $800 million on a "fully funded plan" just nine months earlier. An Exodus executive later joked to me: "When we drove off the cliff, we left no skid marks." If Exodus could lose $50 billion in market capitalization and $800 million in cash that fast, I needed a backup plan.

In my first attempt at a "Plan B," we evaluated acquiring Data Return, a company like ours that focused more on Windows applications than Unix applications as we did. We studied the deal for weeks, modeling what the two companies might look like together, figuring out product offerings and cost synergies. My CFO at the time was extremely excited about the deal since it would make use of his favorite skill set—cost cutting.

Toward the end of the process, I took a two-day vacation to Ashland, Oregon. Almost as soon as I arrived, I received an urgent call from John O'Farrell, who was in charge of corporate and business development.

John: "Ben, sorry to disturb you on vacation, but we just had a meeting on the Data Return deal and I don't think that we should do it."

Ben: "Why not?"

John: "Quite frankly, our business is in trouble and their business is in trouble and putting them together will just be double trouble."

Ben: "I was thinking the exact same thing."

In fact, looking at Data Return's business made it crystal clear to me that Loudcloud would probably not end well. Some things are much easier to see in others than in yourself. Looking at Data Return, I could see Loudcloud's future, and it was not pretty. I had a great deal of trouble sleeping as I thought about our fate. I tried to make myself feel better by asking, "What's the worst thing that could happen?" The answer always came back the same: "We'll go bankrupt, I'll lose everybody's money including my mother's, I'll have to lay off all the people who have been working so hard in a very bad economy, all of the customers who trusted me will be screwed, and my reputation will be ruined." Funny, asking that question never made me feel any better.

Then one day I asked myself a different question: "What would I do if we went bankrupt?" The answer that I came up with surprised me: "I'd buy our software, Opsware, which runs in Loudcloud, out of bankruptcy and start a software company." Opsware was the software that we'd written to automate all the tasks of running the cloud: provisioning servers and networking equipment, deploying applications, recovering the environment in case of disaster, and so forth. Then I asked myself another question: "Is there a way to do that without going bankrupt?"

I ran through different scenarios in my mind where we might move into the software business and exit the cloud business. In each scenario, step one was separating Opsware from Loudcloud. Opsware had been written to run only in Loudcloud and had many constraints that prevented it from being a product that would work in any environment. I asked my cofounder and CTO Tim Howes how long it would take to separate Opsware from Loudcloud. He said about nine months, which would prove to be quite optimistic. I immediately assigned a team of ten engineers to start the process in a project we called Oxide.

At this point, our business was still a cloud business, and I gave no indication to the rest of the staff that I might have other ideas. Doing so would have instantly doomed the only business we were in, as everyone would want to work on the future and not the past. I said that Oxide was simply another product line. This statement deeply worried two of my employees who had graduated from Stanford Business School. They scheduled an appointment and presented me with a slide deck detailing why my decision to start Oxide was quixotic, misguided, and downright stupid. They argued that it would steal precious resources from our core business while pursuing a product that would surely fail. I let them present all forty-five slides without my asking them a single question. When they finished I said, "Did I ask for this presentation?" Those were the first words I spoke as I made the transition from a peacetime CEO to a wartime CEO.

By virtue of my position and the fact that we were a public company, nobody besides me had the complete picture. I knew we were in deep, deep trouble. Nobody besides me could get us out of the trouble, and I was through listening to advice about what we should do from people who did not understand all the pieces. I wanted all the data and information I could get, but I didn't need any recommendations about the future direction of the company. This was wartime. The company would live or die by the quality of my decisions, and there was no way to hedge or soften the responsibility. If everybody I had hired—and who gave their lives to the company—could be sent home with little to show for it, then there were no excuses that would help. There would be no: "It was a horrible economic environment"; "I got bad advice"; "Things changed so quickly." The only choices were survival or total destruction. Yes, most things could still be delegated and most managers would be empowered to make decisions in their areas of expertise, but the fundamental question of whether—and *how*—Loudcloud could survive was mine and mine alone to answer.

We muddled through the fourth quarter of 2001 and beat our target for the year, delivering $57 million in revenue against our $55 million forecast. Not a great win, but very few companies met expectations that year, so I took it as a small victory. The stock price slowly rose to $4 a share, and it looked as though we might be able to make the cloud business work.

In order to do so, we needed more cash. We carefully analyzed our financial plan and decided that we needed another $50 million to get to cash flow breakeven—the point at which we would no longer need to raise money. Given our momentum in the market, raising money was now barely possible and the only way to do it was in the form of a seldom-used construct called a private investment in public equity (PIPE). We worked with Morgan Stanley to line up investors with the goal of raising $50 million.

It was Monday morning, and we were all set to hit the road on Tuesday to raise the PIPE when I got the call. "Ben, the CEO of Atriax is on the phone; shall I put him through?" Atriax, an online foreign currency exchange backed by Citibank and Deutsche Bank, was our largest customer. Atriax paid us more than $1 million per month and had a two-year guaranteed contract. I was in the middle of a meeting with Deb Casados, my vice president of human resources, but I said, "Put him through." He then informed me that Atriax was bankrupt and could not pay any of the $25 million he owed us. It was like the world stopped spinning. I sat there in a daze until I heard Deb's voice saying, "Ben, Ben, Ben, do you want to have this meeting later?" I said, "Yep." I walked slowly over to my CFO's office to assess the damage. It was worse than I thought.

Given the materiality of losing the contract, we could not raise money without first disclosing that we'd lost our largest customer and $25 million out of our financial plan. We put the PIPE road show on hold and then issued a press release. The stock immediately fell by 50 percent, and with a rapidly declining market cap of $160 million, we could no longer raise $50 million in a PIPE. The plan that was $50 million short of breakeven was now, with the loss of Atriax, $75 million short of breakeven with no way to close the gap. Loudcloud was doomed. I had to deploy Oxide.

The situation was complex, because 440 of our 450 employees worked in the cloud business, which represented all of our customers and generated 100 percent of our revenue. I could not tell the employees or even my executive team that I was considering abandoning the cloud business, because our stock price would have collapsed to nothing, killing any hope of selling the company and avoiding bankruptcy.

The one person I needed and could trust was John O'Farrell. John ran business and corporate development, but more than that he was the greatest big-deal person I had ever known. To illustrate my point, let's say you were a religious man. We're speaking in the hypothetical now. And let's say you had reached your end of days and you faced your maker for final judgment. Let's further suppose that as your fate was to be decided for all eternity, you were granted a single person to negotiate on your behalf. Whom would you choose? Well, if it were me, I'd take that Irish brother, John O'Farrell.

I told John that he and I needed to execute a contingency plan, and we needed to get started immediately. This would be a two-person project to start, and we needed everyone else focused on the task at hand—reducing Loudcloud's cash burn. Next I called Bill Campbell to explain why I thought we needed to exit the cloud business.

Bill understood what a crisis looked like since he'd been CEO of GO Corporation in the early 1990s. Essentially GO had attempted to build an iPhone-like device in 1992 and ended up being one of the largest venture capital losses in history. I took Bill through my logic: The only way out of the cloud business without going bankrupt was through higher sales, because even if we laid off 100 percent of the employees, the infrastructure costs would still kill us without a sharper sales ramp. I further explained that the dwindling cash balance decreased customer confidence, which in turn hurt sales, which in turn caused the cash balance to decline further. He simply said "spiral." And I knew that he understood.

John and I mapped out the ecosystem to figure out which companies might be interested in acquiring the Loudcloud business. Unfortunately, many of the prospective buyers were in dire straits themselves. Giant telecoms Qwest and WorldCom were embroiled in accounting fraud cases, and Exodus had already gone bankrupt. We decided to focus on the three most likely buyers: IBM, Cable & Wireless, and EDS.

IBM's hosting business, led by the congenial Jim Corgel, immediately took a strong interest. Jim valued the Loudcloud brand and our reputation for technological superiority. EDS, on the other hand, showed no interest. This worried me intensely as I studied all the public filings from both companies; it was clear to me that EDS needed Loudcloud far more than IBM did. Needs always trump wants in mergers and acquisitions. John said to me, "Ben, I think we need to walk away from EDS, so that we can focus on the higher-probability targets." I asked him to draw the EDS organizational chart one more time to see if we could find someone influential at EDS whom we hadn't yet approached. When he did, I asked, "Who is Jeff Kelly?" John paused, then said, "You know, we haven't gotten to Jeff, but he may be able to make this decision."

Sure enough, Jeff was interested. Now with two potential bidders, we put things in motion. John and I worked hard to create urgency with both IBM and EDS, because time was against us. We hosted both companies in our facilities, sometimes with them passing each other in the hallway as part of John's well-orchestrated sales technique. The final step was to set the timeline for the endgame. John and I debated the best way to do this as the deadlines that we planned to set were clearly artificial. I suggested that we stop by Los Angeles on our way to Plano, Texas, home of EDS, to get some advice from Michael Ovitz.

Michael was on Loudcloud's board, but more important, he had formerly been known by many observers as the Most Powerful Man in Hollywood. When he was twenty-eight years old, he started a talent agency, Creative Artists Agency (CAA), which grew to dominate the entertainment industry. CAA's rise made Michael so influential that he could routinely structure deals that had never been done before.

When we arrived in his offices, the place buzzed with activity. Michael seemed to be engaged in a dozen different activities, but finally came out to meet with John and me. We explained the situation: We were racing against time and had two bidders, but no specific incentive to coax them toward the end of the process. Michael paused, thought for a moment, and then delivered his advice:

"Gentlemen, I've done many deals in my lifetime and through that process, I've developed a methodology, a way of doing things, a philosophy if you will. Within that philosophy, I have certain beliefs. I believe in artificial deadlines. I believe in playing one against the other. I believe in doing everything and anything short of illegal or immoral to get the damned deal done."

Michael had a way of making things extremely clear.

We thanked him and headed to the airport. We called both EDS and IBM to let them know that we would complete the process over the next eight weeks and sell the Loudcloud business to someone. If they wanted to play, they had to move on that schedule or withdraw immediately. The Michael Ovitz artificial deadline was in full effect. We knew that we might have to go past it, but Michael gave us confidence that going past the deadline was a better move than not having one.

After seven weeks, we came to an agreement with EDS. They would buy Loudcloud for $63.5 million in cash and assume its associated liabilities and cash burn. We would retain the intellectual property, Opsware, and become a software company. EDS would then license our software to run both Loudcloud and the larger EDS for $20 million per year. I thought it was a great deal for both EDS and us. It was certainly far better than bankruptcy. I felt 150 pounds lighter. I could take a deep breath for the first time in eighteen months.

Still, it wouldn't be easy. Selling Loudcloud meant selling about 150 employees to EDS and laying off another 140.

I called Bill Campbell to tell him the good news: The deal was signed and we would be announcing it in New York on Monday. He replied, "Too bad you can't go to New York and be part of the announcement; you'll have to send Marc." I said, "What do you mean?" He said, "You need to stay home and make sure everybody knows where they stand. You can't wait a day. In fact, you can't wait a minute. They need to know whether they are working for you, EDS, or looking for a fucking job." Damn. He was right. I sent Marc to New York and prepared to let people know where they stood. That small piece of advice from Bill proved to be the foundation we needed to rebuild the company. If we hadn't treated the people who were leaving fairly, the people who stayed would never have trusted me again. Only a CEO who had been through some awful, horrible, devastating circumstances would know to give that advice at that time.

# CHAPTER 3

# THIS TIME WITH FEELING

"I move onward, the only direction
Can't be scared to fail in search of perfection."
JAY Z, "ON TO THE NEXT ONE"

Once the EDS sale was completed, I felt like the company was in good shape, but my shareholders did not agree. I had sold all of my customers, all of my revenue, and the business they understood. Every large shareholder bailed out, and the stock price fell to $0.35 per share, which represented about half of the cash we had in the bank. I realized that nobody besides me knew how bad things had become and nobody besides me believed in the future, so I decided to take the employees off-site and resell them on the opportunity.

I rented forty rooms in a low-end motel in Santa Cruz and took our remaining eighty employees there for one night of drinking and one day of explaining the Opsware opportunity. At the end of the day, I tried to be as honest as humanly possible.

"You have now heard everything that I know and think about the opportunity in front of us. Wall Street does not believe Opsware is a good idea, but I do. I can understand if you don't. Since this is a brand-new company and a brand-new challenge, I am issuing everyone new stock grants today. All that I ask is that if you have decided to quit that you quit today. I won't walk you out the door—I'll help you find a job. But, we need to know where we stand. We need to know who is with us and whom we can count on. We cannot afford to slowly bleed out. You owe it to your teammates to be honest. Let us know where you stand."

That day two employees quit. Of the other seventy-eight, all but two stayed through the sale to Hewlett-Packard five years later.

After the off-site gathering, the first thing I had to do was increase the stock price. The NASDAQ had sent me a curt letter stating that if we failed to get our stock price over a dollar, they would "delist" us from the exchange and send us to the purgatory known as penny stocks. The board debated the best way to do this— reverse-split the stock, a stock buyback, or other options—but I felt we just needed to tell our story. The story was simple. We had a great team, $60 million in the bank, a $20 million a year contract with EDS, and some serious intellectual property. Unless I was the worst CEO of all time, we should be worth more than $30 million. The story took hold, and the stock climbed above $1 a share.

Next, I had to ship a product. Opsware had been built to run Loudcloud and Loudcloud only. It was not yet ready for the world. In fact, parts of the code were hardwired to physical machines in our building. Beyond that, the user interface was far from ready for prime time. The component that managed the network was called the Jive and featured a purple pimp hat on the front page. Project Oxide gave us a running start, but our engineers were nervous. They brought me a long list of features that they felt we needed to complete prior to entering the market. They pointed to competitors with more finished products.

As I listened to their lengthy objections, it became clear to me that the features the engineers wanted to add all came from Loudcloud requirements. As painful as it might be, I knew that we had to get into the broader market in order to understand it well enough to build the right product. Paradoxically, the only way to do that was to ship and try to sell the wrong product. We would fall on our faces, but we would learn fast and do what was needed to survive.

Finally, I had to rebuild the executive team. I had a CFO who didn't know software accounting, a head of sales who had never sold software, and a head of marketing who did not know our market. Every one of them was great at their old jobs, but not qualified for their new jobs. It was miserable, but necessary, to see them all go.

The strategy and the team came together, and the business started working. We began signing customers at a consistent pace and our stock price rose from its $0.35 low to more than $7 a share. It felt like we were finally out of the woods.

Naturally I was wrong.

## SIXTY DAYS TO LIVE

A few quarters into Opsware, we received very bad news from our largest customer, EDS. "Largest customer" really understates it; EDS accounted for 90 percent of our revenue. And they were not happy. Their Opsware deployment had stalled out and not met its goals as they had run into multiple difficult technical issues. EDS wanted to cancel the deployment, end the contract, and get their money back. Giving EDS their money back would mean the end of Opsware. Getting into a big dispute with a customer that accounted for all but 10 percent of our revenue would also mean the end of Opsware. We were doomed again.

I called my top two lieutenants on the account in for a meeting.

Jason Rosenthal was the very first employee I had hired and the best manager in the company. A Stanford graduate with an impeccable memory and a genius mind for managing all the details of a complex project, Jason was in charge of the EDS deployment.

Anthony Wright grew up in the tough part of Pittsburgh, the son of legendary street fighter Joe Wright, and had earned a black belt in several martial arts himself. Self-made, super-determined, and unwilling to fail, Anthony had an uncanny ability to quickly gain deep insight into people's character and motivations—"able to charm dogs off a meat truck," is how another guy on the team described it. Anthony was the relationship manager for EDS.

I began with an assessment: What happened? It turned out, a lot of things. EDS's environment was insane and chaotic. They had inherited networks and infrastructure from every customer they'd ever signed and from every era in which they had signed them. They had data centers connected by 56-kilobit links at a time when no other customer connected at speeds even twenty times that slow. EDS ran versions of operating systems that were so old that they didn't support basic technologies like threads, which meant our software wouldn't run on them. And the people were not our people. We'd find them sleeping in the data center at two o'clock in the afternoon; they were not motivated and generally not very happy. Beyond that, our product was far from perfect and every one of the many bugs and shortcomings was a reason to stop the deployment.

I took a long pause, rubbed my head, and then began to give instructions. I chose my words carefully:

"I appreciate the difficulties and more than that, I thank you deeply for the effort. However, I do not think that I've made myself clear on the situation that we're in. This is not a scenario where an excuse will do. This is a must win. If EDS drops us, we're fucked and it's over. The IPO, avoiding the Loudcloud bankruptcy, all the layoffs and pain will have been for nothing—because we're dead. So, our only option is to win. We cannot lose this one.

"Jason, the whole company is at your command. Whatever you need, I will make sure you get it. Anthony, Jason is going to work to deliver all the value that EDS expects, but he will fail. He will fail to deliver one hundred percent of expectations, so you are now in charge of finding out what they don't expect, but want. You are in charge of finding the exciting value. When you do, we will deliver it."

Jason and Anthony then headed to Plano, Texas, to meet with their counterparts at EDS.

They didn't know who was making decisions, but after a bunch of meetings and dead ends, they found their way to the office of a person I will call Frank Johnson (not his real name)—a big guy who grew up in the oil fields of Oklahoma, graduated from West Point, and now was in charge of anyone who touched any servers at EDS. Anthony and Jason touted the Opsware technology and potential cost savings.

After listening for a bit, Frank pushed back his chair, stood up, and shouted, "You fucking want to know what I think about Opsware? I think it's the biggest goddamn piece of shit! All I hear about all day is how much this product fucking sucks. I'm going to do everything I can to get you guys thrown out of here."

Frank revealed his plan to remove all of our software immediately, demanding all funds to be returned. He was dead serious.

Anthony remained calm, looked him in the eye, and said, "Frank, I will do exactly as you say. I've heard you loud and clear. This is a terrible moment for you and for us. Allow me to use your phone, and I will call Ben Horowitz and give him your instructions. But before I do, can I ask you one thing? If my company made the commitment to fix these issues, how much time would you give us to do that?"

He responded, "Sixty days." Anthony told him the clock had just started ticking and left his office immediately. It was good news: We had exactly sixty days to fix all the problems and make the deployment work. If we did not, we were done. We had sixty days to live.

An early lesson I learned in my career was that whenever a large organization attempts to do anything, it always comes down to a single person who can delay the entire project. An engineer might get stuck waiting for a decision or a manager may think she doesn't have authority to make a critical purchase. These small, seemingly minor hesitations can cause fatal delays. I could not afford any hesitation, so I scheduled a daily meeting with Anthony, Jason, and the team— though they were now based in Plano. The purpose was to remove all roadblocks. If anyone was stuck on anything for any reason, it could not last more than twenty-four hours—the time between meetings.

Meanwhile, Anthony worked furiously to find the exciting value we could offer EDS. We started with little things that did not change our fate, but revealed important clues. We flew our main EDS executive, Frank, out to meet with our top engineers and architects. In booking the trip, Anthony reported that Frank requested the longest layover possible in the connecting airport. I thought that I misheard him. "What, he wants a long layover?"

Anthony: "Yep."

Ben: "Why would anybody want a long layover in an airport?"

Anthony: "Apparently, he likes to hang out in the airport bar between flights."

Ben: "Why does he like to do that?"

Anthony: "I asked him the same question. Frank said: 'Because I hate my job and I hate my family.'"

Wow. I had no idea who I was dealing with until that point. Understanding how differently Frank viewed the world than the people at Opsware helped clarify my thoughts. Frank expected to get screwed by us. It's what always happened to him in his job and presumably in his personal life. We needed something dramatic to break his psychology. We needed to be associated with the airport bar, not with his job or his family.

At the same time, Jason marched the team through the deployment with unrelenting precision. A month into the plan, the Southwest Airlines crew that worked the San Jose–Dallas flight knew Jason and his team by name. They made steady progress, but it wasn't going to be enough. We would not get EDS fully deployed in sixty days—so now we really needed Anthony to deliver exciting value.

As I sat in my office hoping for a breakthrough, my cell phone rang. It was Anthony.

Anthony: "Ben, I think I've got it."

Ben: "Got what?"

Anthony: "The exciting value is Tangram."

Ben: "What?"

Anthony: "Tangram. EDS uses a product from a company called Tangram that inventories their hardware and software. Frank absolutely loves it, but the purchasing guys are going to force him to switch to an equivalent Computer Associates product, because it's free as part of EDS's settlement with CA. Frank hates the CA product. Frank is getting screwed again."

Ben: "So what can we do?"

Anthony: "If Tangram can come free with Opsware, then Frank will love us."

Ben: "That sounds economically impossible. If we buy the licenses from Tangram and give them to EDS, that will be a colossal expense. We'll never be able to describe it to Wall Street."

Anthony: "You asked me what EDS really wanted. They really want Tangram."

Ben: "Got it."

I had never heard of Tangram, so I quickly looked them up. They were a small company in Cary, North Carolina, but they traded on the NASDAQ market. I looked up their market capitalization. This couldn't be right. Tangram Enterprise Solutions, according to Yahoo Finance, was worth only $6 million. I had never heard of a public company being that cheap.

I immediately called my head of business development, John O'Farrell, and told him that I wanted to buy Tangram, and I needed the entire process to be extremely quick—as in, I wanted the Tangram acquisition done before our sixty-day window with EDS closed.

Tangram was run by Norm Phelps, an interim CEO, which was a great sign that they'd be willing to sell the company, because most boards would much rather sell a company than roll the dice by hiring a new CEO. John got in touch with Tangram and they were immediately interested, so we assembled a team to conduct due diligence while we negotiated a merger agreement in parallel. At the end of due diligence, I brought my team back together. They promptly and unanimously agreed that buying Tangram would be a bad idea: The technology would be difficult to integrate and not that valuable. The company was in North Carolina. It was fifteen years old and the technology was old, too. The finance team thought the acquisition was a money loser. I listened, and then I told them all that I didn't care about any of that. We were going to buy Tangram. The team seemed shocked, but did not argue with me.

John and I negotiated a deal to buy Tangram for $10 million in cash and stock. We signed the deal prior to the end of the sixty-day plan. I called Frank from EDS to tell him that once the transaction closed, we would include all Tangram software for free as part of his Opsware contract. Frank was ecstatic. Now that we had solved Frank's Tangram problem, he viewed the work that Jason's team completed in a totally different light. At the end of the sixty days, Frank gathered our team and made the following speech:

"I've given the speech that I gave to you guys at the beginning of this process to at least a dozen other vendors. They all promised things, but none ever delivered. You guys really delivered and I am shocked. You are the best vendor that I have and I am happy to be working with you."

We'd done it. We saved the account and saved the company. What a relief! But we still had the small matter of the company that we'd just purchased and its fifty-seven employees. Some decisions were simple—we didn't need nine out of the ten salespeople, because they weren't selling anything. Some were more complex: Should we keep the North Carolina location? In the end, we decided to keep it and locate customer support there. It turned out that when you accounted for turnover rates and the cost of recruiting and training, Cary, North Carolina, engineers were cheaper to hire than Bangalore, India, engineers. As the years went by, Tangram proved to be a highly profitable acquisition—well beyond the critical role it played in saving the EDS account.

During acquisition talks, both sides had agreed that Tangram's CFO, John Nelli, would not become part of Opsware. But during the time between signing and close, John began to get severe headaches. His doctors discovered that he had brain cancer. Because he would not be an Opsware employee and it was a preexisting condition, he would not be eligible for health insurance under our plan. The cost of the treatment without health insurance would likely bankrupt his family. I asked my head of HR what it would cost to keep him on the payroll long enough to qualify for COBRA and what COBRA would cost. It wasn't cheap—about $200,000. This was a significant amount of money for a company in our situation. On top of that, we barely knew John and technically we didn't "owe" him anything. This wasn't our problem. We were fighting for our lives.

We were fighting for our lives, but he was about to lose his. I decided to pay for his health costs and find the money elsewhere in the budget. I never expected to hear anything else about that decision, but fifteen months later I received a handwritten letter from John's wife letting me know that John had died. She wrote that she was absolutely shocked that I would help a total stranger and his family and that I had saved her from total despair. She went on for several paragraphs saying that she didn't know why I did it, but it enabled her to continue living and she was eternally grateful.

I guess I did it because I knew what desperation felt like.

## SURVIVAL OF THE FITTEST

Almost as soon as the EDS crisis was resolved, I got news that three new clients we had expected to sign were now fading away. An excellent new competitor, BladeLogic, had arisen and was beating us in key accounts. We lost several deals to them and missed our quarterly numbers as a result. The stock price dropped back down to $2.90.

Here we go again.

With a losing product, a dwindling stock price, and a tired team, I knew we were in trouble. To make matters worse, Marc, who had been working exclusively with me on Loudcloud and Opsware as "full-time chairman of the board," had decided to found another company, Ning. The success or failure of Opsware was really up to the team and me at this point, but the timing sucked. Not only was the company circling the drain, but our most visible spokesman was going to work on something else. Damn. After all that we had been through, how could I ask the team to charge up yet another impossible mountain? How could I muster the strength to do it myself?

I felt like I had no more stories, no more speeches, and no more "rah-rah" in me. I decided to level with the team and see what happened. I called an all engineering meeting and gave the following speech:

"I have some bad news. We are getting our asses kicked by Blade-Logic and it's a product problem. If this continues, I am going to have to sell the company for cheap. There is no way for us to survive if we don't have the winning product. So, I am going to need every one of you to do something. I need you to go home tonight and have a serious conversation with your wife, husband, significant other, or whoever cares most about you and tell them, 'Ben needs me for the next six months.' I need you to come in early and stay late. I will buy you dinner, and I will stay here with you. Make no mistake, we have one bullet left in the gun and we must hit the target."

At the time, I felt horrible asking the team to make yet another big sacrifice. Amazingly, I found out while writing this book that I probably should have felt good about it. Here's what Ted Crossman, one of my best engineers, said about that time and the launch of the aptly named Darwin Project many years later:

*Of all the times I think of at Loudcloud and Opsware, the Darwin Project was the most fun and the most hard. I worked seven days a week 8 a.m.–10 p.m. for six months straight. It was full on. Once a week I had a date night with my wife where I gave her my undivided attention from 6 p.m. until midnight. And the next day, even if it was Saturday, I'd be back in the office at 8 a.m. and stay through dinner. I would come home between 10–11 p.m. Every night. And it wasn't just me. It was everybody in the office.*

*The technical things asked of us were great. We had to brainstorm how to do things and translate those things into an actual product.*

*It was hard, but fun. I don't remember losing anyone during that time. It was like, "Hey, we gotta get this done, or we will not be here, we'll have to get another job." It was a tight-knit group of people. A lot of the really junior people really stepped up. It was a great growing experience for them to be thrown into the middle of the ocean and told, "Okay, swim."*

*Six months later we suddenly started winning proofs of concepts we hadn't before. Ben did a great job, he'd give us feedback, and pat people on the back when we were done.*

Eight years later, when I read what Ted had written, I cried. I cried because I didn't know. I thought I did, but I really didn't. I thought that I was asking too much of everybody. I thought that after barely surviving Loudcloud, nobody was ready for another do-or-die mission. I wish I knew then what I know now.

After the speech came the hard work of defining the product. The product plan was weighed down with hundreds of requirements from our existing customers. The product management team had an allergic reaction to prioritizing potentially good features above features that might hypothetically beat BladeLogic. They would say, "How can we walk away from requirements that we *know* to be true to pursue something that we *think* will help?"

It turns out that is exactly what product strategy is all about—figuring out the right product is the innovator's job, not the customer's job. The customer only knows what she thinks she wants based on her experience with the current product. The innovator can take into account everything that's possible, but often must go against what she *knows* to be true. As a result, innovation requires a combination of knowledge, skill, and courage. Sometimes only the founder has the courage to ignore the data; we were running out of time, so I had to step in:

"I don't care about any of the existing requirements; I need you to reinvent the product and we need to win." Nine months later, when we released our new product we could now win any deal. Armed with the new product, Mark Cranney, head of sales, went to war.

After assembling a top-end sales force, he completely revamped the sales process and sent every salesperson through a rigorous and unforgiving training program. He demanded mastery. Any slip-up in technique, skill, or knowledge would be met with total intolerance from Mark.

We held a weekly forecast call where Mark reviewed every deal in front of the entire 150 person sales force. On one such call, a salesperson described an account that he'd forecast in detail: "I have buy-in from my champion, the vice president that he reports to, and the head of purchasing. My champion assures me that they'll be able to complete the deal by the end of the fiscal quarter."

Mark quickly replied, "Have you spoken to the vice president's peer in the networking group?"

Sales rep: "Um, no I haven't."

Mark: "Have you spoken to the vice president yourself?"

Sales rep: "No."

Mark: "Okay, listen carefully. Here's what I'd like you to do. First, reach up to your face and take off your rose-colored glasses. Then get a Q-tip and clean the wax out of your ears. Finally, take off your pink panties and call the fucking vice president right now, because you do not have a deal."

Mark was right. It turned out that we did not have a deal, as the vice president's peer in networking was blocking it. We eventually got a meeting with him and won the deal. More important, Mark set the tone: Sloppiness would not be tolerated.

Now that we'd improved our competitive position, we went on the offensive. In my weekly staff meeting, I inserted an agenda item titled "What Are We Not Doing?" Ordinarily in a staff meeting, you spend lots of time reviewing, evaluating, and improving all of the things that you do: build products, sell products, support customers, hire employees, and the like. Sometimes, however, the things you're not doing are the things you should actually be focused on.

In one such meeting, after asking the question, every person on my staff agreed: "We are not automating the network." Although the original version of Opsware that we used in Loudcloud automated our network, the software was not robust and, of course, featured the purple-pimp-hat user interface. As a result, when we switched over to being a software company, we narrowed our focus to server automation and never revisited the decision. This worked well for the first several years of Opsware, but now we had an opportunity to bring back our network automation product.

Unfortunately, the Jive was not a good code base and could not be turned into a commercial product. My choices were: (a) start a new project or (b) buy one of the four existing network automation companies. Early in my career as an engineer, I'd learned that all decisions were objective until the first line of code was written. After that, all decisions were emotional. In addition, I had John O'Farrell, the industry's greatest M&A negotiator, on my team so I decided to investigate the other companies before sizing the internal effort.

Surprisingly, among the four existing network automation players, the company that we thought had the best product architecture, Rendition Networks, had the lowest revenues. This made some of our businesspeople skeptical of our technical evaluation. However, if I'd learned anything it was that conventional wisdom had nothing to do with the truth and the efficient market hypothesis was deceptive. How else could one explain Opsware trading at half of the cash we had in the bank when we had a $20 million a year contract and fifty of the smartest engineers in the world? No, markets weren't "efficient" at finding the truth; they were just very efficient at converging on a conclusion—often the wrong conclusion.

After confirming that acquiring would be superior to building, we negotiated a deal to buy Rendition Networks for $33 million. Within three months of completing the acquisition, John negotiated a deal with Cisco Systems—the world's largest networking company—to resell our product. The deal included an agreement to prepay us $30 million for advanced licenses. As a result, the Cisco deal alone paid more than 90 percent of the acquisition costs.

Note to self: It's a good idea to ask, "What am I not doing?"

## THE ULTIMATE DECISION

As we fielded the broader product line, our momentum steadily grew. From the ashes, we'd built a software business that approached a $150 million revenue run rate. Along with our revenue, our stock price rose from its floor of $0.35 per share as well as we traded between $6 per share and $8 per share, sometimes trading at a market capitalization of more than $800 million.

Still, everything was not rosy. Every quarter was tough, and the competitive and the technology landscapes changed rapidly. A technology called virtualization was taking the market by storm and changing the way customers thought about automating their environments. In fact, it looked to me like virtualization might be the technological breakthrough that finally enabled the cloud computing business model to work. Beyond that, being a public company was still never going to get easy. At one point, a shareholder activist named Rachel Hyman decided that my ego was out of control, and she demanded that the board remove me and sell the company immediately. This was despite the fact that we were trading at $7 per share, which was ten times the original price of her shares.

Nonetheless, I was not looking for the exits. Whenever a potential acquirer approached us, I would always reply, "We are not for sale." It was a great answer in that I wasn't ready to sell and it conveyed that, but it also left the door open to a particularly aggressive buyer. "Not for sale" didn't mean that we wouldn't listen to offers—it just meant that we weren't trying to sell the company. So, when EMC implied that it wanted to buy us, I thought nothing of it. We were trading at about $6.50 per share and I wasn't planning to sell at anything close to that price. But this time the news of the offer leaked to the press and the stock shot up to $9.50 per share, changing the economic equation, especially since the stock was going up for all the wrong reasons.

Ironically, the higher the stock price went up, the more companies wanted to buy us. Over the course of the next month, eleven companies expressed interest. Given the uncertainty in the business and the implied earnings multiple, their interest was too much to ignore.

To get things started, John and I called Michael Ovitz to get some advice. We felt one of the potential bidders, Oracle, would be the least likely to bid high, because it was extremely disciplined in its financial analysis. We conveyed this to Michael and questioned whether we should pursue Oracle at all. His reply was priceless: "Well, boys, if you are going to have a dog race, then you are going to need a rabbit. And Oracle will be one hell of a rabbit."

With that strategy in hand, we generated a broad set of bids, all between $10 and $11 per share, with the highest bids representing a 38 percent premium over the current stock price. Although this was considered a good premium, I did not feel right selling the company for $11 per share. The team had worked too hard, we'd accomplished too much, and we were too good a company. The risks of staying stand-alone were substantial, but I still wanted to bet on the team. I recommended to the board that we not sell.

The board was surprised, but supportive. Still, they had a fiduciary responsibility to shareholders to ask the tough questions. "If you're unwilling to sell at eleven dollars per share, is there a price at which you would sell?" I had to think about that one. I had promised the team that if we got to be the number-one company in a big market, we would not sell. We were number one, but how big was the market? Did the team really want to continue or was it just me who wanted to continue? How could I know without panicking the company? And thus began a series of very long talks with myself.

It was an argument to the death, and it was me against me. On the one hand, I argued that virtualization created an explosion of virtual server instances, making what we did more essential than ever. In the next breath, I retorted that while that may have been true, the architectural changes would make our market position vulnerable. I battled myself for weeks before concluding that things were changing fast enough that we'd need to make major changes to our product architecture in order to stay on top. The key to answering the ultimate question was knowing the state of the team. Were they up for yet another giant challenge or were they at the end of a very long road? I decided to bring my direct reports into the loop and ask them what they thought. The answers came back clear: Everyone, with the exception of one person who felt that the opportunity in front of us was still quite large, opted for the sale. Now it was just a matter of price. But what price?

After a long discussion with John O'Farrell, I decided that the right price to sell the company would be $14 per share, or about $1.6 billion. I took that number back to the board. They thought the number was extremely high and that it was unlikely we'd be able to generate a bid at that level, but they were supportive nonetheless. I called back all the potential acquirers and let them know that we would only entertain bids of $14 or more. There were no takers.

More than a month passed without a word, and I figured the M&A talks had ended. I began refocusing on how to make the necessary changes to keep us competitive. And then I received a call from Bob Beauchamp, the CEO of BMC Software. He offered $13.25 per share. I held firm: "Bob, that's great, but the number is fourteen dollars per share." Bob said that he'd have to think about it. He called back two days later and offered $14 per share. Wow. The dog had caught the bus.

John and I immediately called back all the other suitors to let them know that we had an offer that we planned to take. Hewlett-Packard was still interested and offered $13.50 per share in an effort to make sure that I wasn't bluffing. I responded that as a public company CEO, I couldn't take a lower offer. HP eventually offered $14.25 or $1.65 billion in cash. We had a deal.

When it finally ended—the long road from Loudcloud to Opsware—I couldn't believe that I'd sold what it took eight years and all of my life force to build. How could I have done that? I was sick. I couldn't sleep, I had cold sweats, I threw up, and I cried. And then I realized that it was the smartest thing that I'd ever done in my career. We'd built something from nothing, saw it go back to nothing again, and then rebuilt it into a $1.65 billion franchise.

At that point, it felt like my business life was kind of over. I had hired all the best people that I knew or could find, and I had gone through every step from founding to going public to sale. I definitely did not feel like doing any of that again. But I had learned so much. It seemed like such a waste to do something completely different. And then I got an idea to build a new kind of venture capital firm.

We will explore this idea in chapter 9, but first, chapters 4 through 8 will take you through most everything I learned to this point plus a few new war stories from my experiences running Loudcloud and Opsware.

# CHAPTER 4

# WHEN THINGS FALL APART

"There are several different frameworks one could use to get a handle on the indeterminate vs. determinate question. The math version is calculus vs. statistics. In a determinate world, calculus dominates. You can calculate specific things precisely and deterministically. When you send a rocket to the moon, you have to calculate precisely where it is at all times. It's not like some iterative startup where you launch the rocket and figure things out step by step. Do you make it to the moon? To Jupiter? Do you just get lost in space? There were lots of companies in the '90s that had launch parties but no landing parties.

"But the indeterminate future is somehow one in which probability and statistics are the dominant modality for making sense of the world. Bell curves and random walks define what the future is going to look like. The standard pedagogical argument is that high schools should get rid of calculus and replace it with statistics, which is really important and actually useful. There has been a powerful shift toward the idea that statistical ways of thinking are going to drive the future."

—PETER THIEL

When I was attempting to sell the cloud computing services part of the Loudcloud business, I met with Bill Campbell to update him on where I was with the deal. The deal was critical, because without it, the company would almost certainly go bankrupt.

After I carefully briefed him on where we were with both inter-ested parties, IBM and EDS, Bill paused for a moment. He looked me in the eyes and said, "Ben, you need to do something in addition to working on this deal. You need to do it alone with your general coun-sel. You need to prepare the company for bankruptcy." To an objective observer, this might sound like Bill was prudently advising me to build my contingency plan. But something in his voice and his eyes said something different. They said that he believed the contingency plan was going to be *the* plan.

The conversation brought to mind a story that a friend told me about his brother, a young doctor. A thirty-five-year-old man came to see my friend's brother. The man looked awful. His eyes were hollow and his skin was ashen. The young doctor knew something was wrong, but he could not figure out what, so he brought in an elder colleague to help with the diagnosis. The more experienced doctor examined the man and then sent him on his way. The old doctor then turned to the young doctor and said, "He's dead." The young doctor was flabbergasted: "What are you talking about? He just walked out of here alive!" The older doctor replied, "He doesn't know it yet, but he's dead. He's had a heart attack and when people that young have heart attacks their bodies are not yet pliable enough to recover. He won't recover. He's dead." Three weeks later the patient died.

I felt that Bill was telling me, although I was walking around trying to get the deal done, that I was already dead and that I did not know it. It was a very hard thing for him to say and only the best of friends will muster the courage to break news that horrible. It was an even harder thing for me to hear. He told me so that I could emo-tionally prepare myself and financially prepare the company for the inevitable funeral. The odds of landing a company-saving deal during the technology industry's nuclear winter were close to nil. Chances were, I was dead.

I never built that contingency plan. Through the seemingly impos-sible Loudcloud series C and IPO processes, I learned one important lesson: Startup CEOs should not play the odds. When you are building a company, you must believe there is an answer and you cannot pay attention to your odds of finding it. You just have to find it. It matters not whether your chances are nine in ten or one in a thousand; your task is the same.

In the end, I did find the answer, we completed the deal with EDS, and the company did not go bankrupt. I was not mad at Bill. To this day, I sincerely appreciate his telling me the truth about the odds. But I don't believe in statistics. I believe in calculus.

People always ask me, "What's the secret to being a successful CEO?" Sadly, there is no secret, but if there is one skill that stands out, it's the ability to focus and make the best move when there are no good moves. It's the moments where you feel most like hiding or dying that you can make the biggest difference as a CEO. In the rest of this chapter, I offer some lessons on how to make it through the struggle without quitting or throwing up too much.

While most management books focus on how to do things correctly, so you don't screw up, these lessons provide insight into what you must do after you have screwed up. The good news is, I have plenty of experience at that and so does every other CEO.

I put this section first even though it deals with some serious endgame issues such as how to fire an executive and how to lay people off. In doing so, I follow the first principle of the Bushido—the way of the warrior: keep death in mind at all times. If a warrior keeps death in mind at all times and lives as though each day might be his last, he will conduct himself properly in all his actions. Similarly, if a CEO keeps the following lessons in mind, she will maintain the proper focus when hiring, training, and building her culture.

# THE STRUGGLE

Every entrepreneur starts her company with a clear vision for success. You will create an amazing environment and hire the smartest people to join you. Together you will build a beautiful product that delights customers and makes the world just a little bit better. It's going to be absolutely awesome.

Then, after working night and day to make your vision a reality, you wake up to find that things did not go as planned. Your company did not unfold like the Jack Dorsey keynote that you listened to when you started. Your product has issues that will be very hard to fix. The market isn't quite where it was supposed to be. Your employees are losing confidence and some of them have quit. Some of the ones who quit were quite smart and have the remaining ones wondering if staying makes sense. You are running low on cash and your venture capitalist tells you that it will be difficult to raise money given the impending European economic catastrophe. You lose a competitive battle. You lose a loyal customer. You lose a great employee. The walls start closing in. Where did you go wrong? Why didn't your company perform as envisioned? Are you good enough to do this? As your dreams turn into nightmares, you find yourself in *the Struggle*.

## ABOUT THE STRUGGLE

"Life is struggle."

—KARL MARX

The Struggle is when you wonder why you started the company in the first place.

The Struggle is when people ask you why you don't quit and you don't know the answer.

The Struggle is when your employees think you are lying and you think they may be right.

The Struggle is when food loses its taste.

The Struggle is when you don't believe you should be CEO of your company. The Struggle is when you know that you are in over your head and you know that you cannot be replaced. The Struggle is when everybody thinks you are an idiot, but nobody will fire you. The Struggle is where self-doubt becomes self-hatred.

The Struggle is when you are having a conversation with someone and you can't hear a word that they are saying because all you can hear is the Struggle.

The Struggle is when you want the pain to stop. The Struggle is unhappiness.

The Struggle is when you go on vacation to feel better and you feel worse.

The Struggle is when you are surrounded by people and you are all alone. The Struggle has no mercy.

The Struggle is the land of broken promises and crushed dreams. The Struggle is a cold sweat. The Struggle is where your guts boil so much that you feel like you are going to spit blood.

The Struggle is not failure, but it causes failure. Especially if you are weak. Always if you are weak.

Most people are not strong enough.

Every great entrepreneur from Steve Jobs to Mark Zuckerberg went through the Struggle and struggle they did, so you are not alone. But that does not mean that you will make it. You may not make it. That is why it is the Struggle.

The Struggle is where greatness comes from.

## SOME STUFF THAT MAY OR MAY NOT HELP

There is no answer to the Struggle, but here are some things that helped me:

- *Don't put it all on your shoulders.* It is easy to think that the things that bother you will upset your people more. That's not true. The opposite is true. Nobody takes the losses harder than the person most responsible. Nobody feels it more than you. You won't be able to share every burden, but share every burden that you can. Get the maximum number of brains on the problems even if the problems represent existential threats. When I ran Opsware and we were losing too many competitive deals, I called an all hands and told the whole company that we were getting our asses kicked, and if we didn't stop the bleeding, we were going to die. Nobody blinked. The team rallied, built a winning product, and saved my sorry ass.

- *This is not checkers; this is motherfuckin' chess.* Technology businesses tend to be extremely complex. The underlying technology moves, the competition moves, the market moves, the people move. As a result, like playing three-dimensional chess on *Star Trek*, there is always a move. You think you have no moves? How about taking your company public with $2 million in trailing revenue and 340 employees, with a plan to do $75 million in revenue the next year?

I made that move. I made it in 2001, widely regarded as the worst time ever for a technology company to go public. I made it with six weeks of cash left. There is always a move.

■ *Play long enough and you might get lucky.* In the technology game, tomorrow looks nothing like today. If you survive long enough to see tomorrow, it may bring you the answer that seems so impossible today.

■ *Don't take it personally.* The predicament that you are in is probably all your fault. You hired the people. You made the decisions. But you knew the job was dangerous when you took it. Everybody makes mistakes. Every CEO makes thousands of mistakes. Evaluating yourself and giving yourself an F doesn't help.

■ *Remember that this is what separates the women from the girls.* If you want to be great, this is the challenge. If you don't want to be great, then you never should have started a company.

## THE END

When you are in the Struggle, nothing is easy and nothing feels right. You have dropped into the abyss and you may never get out. In my own experience, but for some unexpected luck and help, I would have been lost.

So to all of you in it, may you find strength and may you find peace.

# CEOS SHOULD TELL IT LIKE IT IS

One of the most important management lessons for a founder/CEO is totally unintuitive. My single biggest personal improvement as CEO occurred on the day when I stopped being too positive.

As a young CEO, I felt the pressure—the pressure of employees depending on me, the pressure of not really knowing what I was doing, the pressure of being responsible for tens of millions of dollars of other people's money. As a consequence of this pressure, I took losses extremely hard. If we failed to win a customer or slipped a date or shipped a product that wasn't quite right, it weighed heavily on me. I thought that I would make the problem worse by transferring that burden to my employees. Instead, I thought I should project a positive, sunny demeanor and rally the unburdened troops to victory. I was completely wrong.

I realized my error during a conversation with my brother in-law, Cartheu. At the time, Cartheu worked for AT&T as a telephone line-man (he is one of those guys who climb the poles). I had just met a senior executive at AT&T, whom I'll call Fred, and I was excited to find out if Cartheu knew him. Cartheu said, "Yeah, I know Fred. He comes by about once a quarter to blow a little sunshine up my ass." At that moment, I knew that I'd been screwing up my company by being too positive.

In my mind, I was keeping everyone in high spirits by accentuating the positive and ignoring the negative. But my team knew that reality was more nuanced than I was describing it. And not only did they see for themselves the world wasn't as rosy as I was describing it; they still had to listen to me blowing sunshine up their butts at every company meeting.

How did I make such a mistake and why was it such a big mistake?

## THE POSITIVITY DELUSION

As the highest-ranking person in the company, I thought that I would be best able to handle bad news. The opposite was true: Nobody took bad news harder than I did. Engineers easily brushed off things that kept me awake all night. After all, I was the founding CEO. I was the one "married" to the company. If things went horribly wrong, they could walk away, but I could not. As a consequence, the employees handled losses much better.

Even more stupidly, I thought that it was my job and my job only to worry about the company's problems. Had I been thinking more clearly, I would have realized that it didn't make sense for me to be the only one to worry about, for example, the product not being quite right—because I wasn't writing the code that would fix it.

A much better idea would have been to give the problem to the people who could not only fix it, but who would also be personally excited and motivated to do so. Another example: If we lost a big prospect, the whole organization needed to understand why, so that we could together fix the things that were broken in our products, marketing, and sales process. If I insisted on keeping the setbacks to myself, there was no way to jump-start that process.

## WHY IT'S IMPERATIVE TO TELL IT LIKE IT IS

There are three key reasons why being transparent about your company's problems makes sense:

### 1. Trust.

Without trust, communication breaks. More specifically:

In any human interaction, the required amount of communication is inversely proportional to the level of trust.

Consider the following: If I trust you completely, then I require no explanation or communication of your actions whatsoever, because I know that whatever you are doing is in my best interests. On the other hand, if I don't trust you at all, then no amount of talking, explaining, or reasoning will have any effect on me, because I do not trust that you are telling me the truth.

In a company context, this is a critical point. As a company grows, communication becomes its biggest challenge. If the employees fundamentally trust the CEO, then communication will be vastly more efficient than if they don't. Telling things as they are is a critical part of building this trust. A CEO's ability to build this trust over time is often the difference between companies that execute well and companies that are chaotic.

### 2. The more brains working on the hard problems, the better.

In order to build a great technology company, you have to hire lots of incredibly smart people. It's a total waste to have lots of big brains but not let them work on your biggest problems. A brain, no matter how big, cannot solve a problem it doesn't know about. As the open-source community would explain it, "Given enough eyeballs, all bugs are shallow."

**3. A good culture is like the old RIP routing protocol: *Bad* news travels fast; good news travels slow.**

If you investigate companies that have failed, you will find that many employees knew about the fatal issues long before those issues killed the company. If the employees knew about the deadly problems, why didn't they say something? Too often the answer is that the company culture discouraged the spread of bad news, so the knowledge lay dormant until it was too late to act.

A healthy company culture encourages people to share bad news. A company that discusses its problems freely and openly can quickly solve them. A company that covers up its problems frustrates everyone involved. The resulting action item for CEOs: Build a culture that rewards—not punishes—people for getting problems into the open where they can be solved.

As a corollary, beware of management maxims that stop information from flowing freely in your company. For example, consider the old management standard: "Don't bring me a problem without bringing me a solution." What if the employee cannot solve an important problem? For example, what if an engineer identifies a serious flaw in the way the product is being marketed? Do you really want him to bury that information? Management truisms like these may be good for employees to aspire to in the abstract, but they can also be the enemy of free-flowing information—which may be critical for the health of the company.

## FINAL THOUGHT

If you run a company, you will experience overwhelming psychological pressure to be overly positive. Stand up to the pressure, face your fear, and tell it like it is.

# THE RIGHT WAY
# TO LAY PEOPLE OFF

Shortly after we sold Opsware to Hewlett-Packard, I had a conversation with the legendary venture capitalist Doug Leone of Sequoia Capital. He wanted me to recount the story of how we went from doomed in the eyes of the world to a $1.6 billion outcome with no recapitalization.

After I took him through the details—including several near bankruptcies, a stock price of $0.35 per share, unlimited bad press, and three separate layoffs where we lost a total of four hundred employees—he was most amazed by the layoffs. During more than twenty years in the venture capital business, he'd never seen a company recover from consecutive layoffs and achieve a billion-dollar-plus outcome. He confessed that he'd bet against that every time. Since my only experience was the great exception, I needed more information. I asked him why all the other startups failed. He replied that the layoffs inevitably broke the company's culture. After seeing their friends laid off, employees were no longer willing to make the requisite sacrifices needed to build a company. He said that although it was possible to survive an isolated layoff, it was hugely unlikely that a company would experience great success. Building a highly valuable business, he added, after three consecutive giant layoffs accompanied by horrible prominent press coverage (we got taken apart with cover stories in both the *Wall Street Journal* and *BusinessWeek*), was a complete violation of the laws of venture capital physics. He wanted to know how we did it. After thinking about this question, here's my answer.

In retrospect, we were able to keep cultural continuity and retain our best employees despite multiple massive layoffs because we laid people off the right way. This may sound nutty—how can you do something that's fundamentally wrong in "the right way"? Here's how.

## STEP 1: GET YOUR HEAD RIGHT

When a company fails to hit its financial plan so severely that it must fire the employees it went to great time and expense to hire, it weighs heavily on the chief executive. During the first layoff at our company, I remember being forwarded an email exchange among a group of employees. In the exchange, one of our smarter employees wrote, "Ben is either lying or stupid or both." I remember reading that and thinking, "definitely stupid." During a time like this, it is difficult to focus on the future, because the past overwhelms you—but that's exactly what you must do.

## STEP 2: DON'T DELAY

Once you decide that you will have to lay people off, the time elapsed between making that decision and executing that decision should be as short as possible. If word leaks (which it will inevitably if you delay), then you will be faced with an additional set of issues. Employees will question managers and ask whether a layoff is coming. If the managers don't know, they will look stupid. If the managers do know, they will either have to lie to their employees, contribute to the leak, or remain silent, which will create additional agitation. At Loudcloud/

Opsware, we badly mismanaged this dynamic with our first round of layoffs, but sharply corrected things on the next two.

## STEP 3: BE CLEAR IN YOUR OWN MIND ABOUT WHY YOU ARE LAYING PEOPLE OFF

Going into a layoff, board members will sometimes try to make you feel better by putting a positive spin on things. They might say, "This gives us a great opportunity to deal with some performance issues and simplify the business." That may be true, but do not let that cloud your thinking or your message to the company. You are laying people off because the company failed to hit its plan. If individual performance were the only issue, then you'd be taking a different measure. *Company* performance failed. This distinction is critical, because the message to the company and the laid-off individuals should not be "This is great, we are cleaning up performance." The message must be "The company failed and in order to move forward, we will have to lose some excellent people." Admitting to the failure may not seem like a big deal, but trust me, it is. "Trust me." That's what a CEO says every day to her employees. Trust me: This will be a good company. Trust me: This will be good for your career. Trust me: This will be good for your life. A layoff breaks that trust. In order to rebuild trust, you have to come clean.

## STEP 4: TRAIN YOUR MANAGERS

The most important step in the whole exercise is training the management team. If you send managers into this super-uncomfortable situation with no training, most of them will fail.

Training starts with a golden rule: *Managers must lay off their own people.* They cannot pass the task to HR or to a more sadistic peer. You cannot hire an outsourcing firm like the one in the movie *Up in the Air.* Every manager must lay off his own people.

Why so strict? Why can't the more confrontational managers just handle this task for everyone? Because people won't remember every day they worked for your company, but they will surely remember the day you laid them off. They will remember every last detail about that day and the details will matter greatly. The reputations of your company and your managers depend on you standing tall, facing the employees who trusted you and worked hard for you. If you hired me and I busted my ass working for you, I expect you to have the courage to lay me off yourself.

Once you make it clear that managers must lay off their own people, be sure to prepare them for the task:

1. They should explain briefly what happened and that it is a company rather than a personal failure.

2. They should be clear that the employee is impacted and that the decision is nonnegotiable.

3. They should be fully prepared with all of the details about the benefits and support the company plans to provide.

## STEP 5: ADDRESS THE ENTIRE COMPANY

Prior to executing the layoff, the CEO must address the company. The CEO must deliver the overall message that provides the proper context and air cover for the managers. If you do your job right, the managers will have a much easier time doing their jobs. Keep in mind what former Intuit CEO Bill Campbell told me—*The message is for the people who are staying.* The people who stay will care deeply about how you treat their colleagues. Many of the people whom you lay off will have closer relationships with the people who stay than you do, so treat them with the appropriate level of respect. Still, the company must move forward, so be careful not to apologize too much.

## STEP 6: BE VISIBLE, BE PRESENT

After you make the speech telling your company that you will be letting many of them go, you will not feel like hanging out and talking to people. You will probably feel like going to a bar and drinking a fifth of tequila. Do not do this. Be present. Be visible. Be engaging. People want to see you. They want to see whether you care. The people whom you laid off will want to know if they still have a relationship with you and the company. Talk to people. Help them carry their things to their cars. Let them know that you appreciate their efforts.

# PREPARING TO FIRE
# AN EXECUTIVE

When you recruit an executive, you paint a beautiful picture of her future in your company. You describe in great depth and in vibrant color how awesome it will be for her to accept your offer and how much better it will be than joining that other company. Then one day you realize you must fire her. Reconcile that, Ms. CEO.

It turns out that the actual act of firing an executive can be relatively easy compared with any other firing. Executives have experience being on the other side of the conversation and tend to be quite professional. Firing an executive correctly is a bit more complicated and extremely important. If you do not learn the right lessons, you will be doing it again soon.

Like so many things, the key to correctly firing an executive is preparation. Here is a four-step process that will treat the executive fairly and improve your company.

## STEP 1: ROOT CAUSE ANALYSIS

While it's possible to fire an executive for bad behavior, incompetence, or laziness, those cases are rare and relatively easy. Unfortunately, unless you have a horribly deficient hiring process, those are probably not the reasons why you got to this point. At this level, almost every company screens for the proper skill set, motivation, and track record. Yes, the reason that you have to fire your head of marketing is not because he sucks; it's because *you* suck.

In other words, the wrong way to view an executive firing is as an executive failure; the correct way to view an executive firing is as an interview/integration process system failure. Therefore, the first step to properly firing an executive is figuring out why you hired the wrong person for your company.

You may have blown it for a variety of reasons:

- *You did a poor job defining the position in the first place.* If you don't know what you want, you will be unlikely to get it. Far too often, CEOs hire executives based on an abstract notion of what they think and feel the executive should be like. This error often leads to the executive not bringing the key, necessary qualities to the table.

- *You hired for lack of weakness rather than for strengths.* This is especially common when you run a consensus-based hiring process. The group will often find the candidate's weaknesses, but they won't place a high enough value on the areas where you need the executive to be a world-class performer. As a result, you hire an executive with no sharp weaknesses, but who is mediocre where you need her to be great. If you don't have world-class strengths where you need them, you won't be a world-class company.

- *You hired for scale too soon.* The most consistently wrong advice that venture capitalists and executive recruiters give CEOs is to hire someone "bigger" than required. "Think about the next three to five years and how you will be a large company" is how the bad advice usually sounds. It's great to hire people who can run a large-scale organization if you have one. It's also great to hire people who know how to grow an organization very fast if you are ready to grow your organization very fast. However, if you do not or you are not, then you need someone who can do the job for the next eighteen months. If you hire someone who will be great *in* eighteen months but will be poor for the next eighteen months, the company will reject her before she ever gets a chance to show her stuff. Your other employees will wonder: Why did we give her all those stock options when she's not contributing anything? Those kinds of questions are impossible to recover from. It turns out that venture capitalists and executive recruiters are not stupid; they just learned the wrong lessons from previous failures. To learn the right lesson, see the *special case of scaling* and *the special case of fast growth* as explained below.

- *You hired for the generic position.* There is no such thing as a great CEO, a great head of marketing, or a great head of sales. There is only a great head of sales for your company for the next twelve to twenty-four months. That position is not the same as the same position at Microsoft or Facebook. Don't look for the candidate out of central casting. This is not a movie.

- *The executive had the wrong kind of ambition.* In chapter 6, I will describe the difference between ambition for the company and ambition for oneself. If an executive has the wrong kind of ambition, then despite her skills, the company may reject her.

- *You failed to integrate the executive.* Bringing a new person into your company in an important role is difficult. Other employees will be quick to judge, her expectations may be different from yours, and the job may be largely undefined.

Be sure to review and improve your integration plan after you fire an executive.

### The special case of scaling

A fairly common reason for firing an executive is that when the company quadruples in size, the executive no longer does the job effectively at the new size. The reason is that when a company multiplies in size, the management jobs become brand-new jobs. As a result, everybody needs to requalify for the new job, because the new job and the old job are not the same. Running a two-hundred-person global sales organization is not the same job as running a twenty-five-person local sales team. If you get lucky, the person you hired to run the twenty-five-person team will have learned how to run the two-hundred-person team. If not, you need to hire the right person for the new job. This is neither an executive failure nor a system failure; it is life in the big city. Do not attempt to avoid this phenomenon, as you will only make things worse.

### The special case of fast growth

If you build a great product and the market wants it, you will find yourself needing to grow your company extremely quickly. Nothing will ensure your success like hiring the right executive who has grown an organization like yours very quickly and successfully before. Note that this is not the same as inheriting a very large organization or working your way up to running a very large organization. Make sure you hire the right kind of fast-growth executive. Also, do not hire this person if you are not ready to give them lots of budget to grow their organization; expect them to do what they do. The successful fast-growth executive is so important to building successful startups that recruiters and venture capitalists often advise CEOs to bring them in before the company is ready.

Once you identify the problem, then you create the basis for the next steps.

## STEP 2: INFORMING THE BOARD

Informing the board is tricky and many issues can further complicate the task:

- This is the fifth or sixth executive that you had to fire.

- This is the third executive that you fired in this role.

- The candidate was referred by a board member who recommended the executive as a superstar.

Realize that in any of these cases the board will be at least somewhat alarmed and there is nothing that you can do about that. But keep in mind that your choices are: (a) alarm the board or (b) enable an ineffective executive to remain in her position. While choice (a) is not great, it's a heck of a lot better than choice (b). Leaving a failing leader in place will cause an entire department in your company to slowly rot. Let that happen and the board will be more than alarmed.

You should have three goals with the board:

- *Get their support and understanding for the difficult task that you will execute.* You should start by making sure that they understand the root cause and your plan to remedy the situation. This will give them confidence in your ability to hire and manage outside executives in the future.

- *Get their input and approval for the separation package.* This will be critical for the next step. Executive packages are larger than regular severance packages and rightly so. It takes about ten times longer for an executive to find a new job than it does for an individual contributor.

■ *Preserve the reputation of the fired executive.* The failure
was very likely a team effort, and it's best to portray it that
way. You don't make yourself look good by trashing someone who worked for you. A mature approach to this issue
will help keep the board confident in your ability to be CEO.
It's also the fair and decent thing to do.

Finally, firing an executive turns out to be a piece of news that's
handled better with individual phone calls than in dramatic fashion
during a board meeting. It takes a bit longer, but it's well worth the
effort. Individual conversations will be particularly important if one
of the board members introduced the executive to the company. Once
everyone agrees individually, you can finalize the details in a board
meeting or call.

## STEP 3: PREPARING FOR THE CONVERSATION

After you know what went wrong and have informed the board, you
should tell the executive as quickly as possible. In preparation for that
meeting, I recommend scripting or rehearsing what you plan to say so
that you do not misspeak. The executive will remember the conversation for a very long time, so you need to get it right.

As part of your preparation, you should review any performance
reviews or written performance conversations to understand any inconsistencies in your prior communication.

Three keys to getting it right:

1. *Be clear on the reasons.* You have thought about this long
   and hard; don't equivocate or sugarcoat it. You owe it to
   them to be clear about what you think happened.

2. *Use decisive language.* Do not leave the discussion open-
   ended. This is not a performance review; it's a firing. Use

words and phrases like "I have decided" rather than "I think."

3. *Have the severance package approved and ready.* Once the executive hears the news, she will stop caring about the company and its issues; she will be highly focused on herself and her family. Be ready to provide specific details of the severance package.

Finally, the executive will be keenly interested in how the news will be communicated to the company and to the outside world. It is best to let her decide. Bill Campbell once gave me a critical bit of advice when I was preparing to fire an executive. He said, "Ben, you cannot let him keep his job, but you absolutely can let him keep his respect."

## STEP 4: PREPARING THE COMPANY COMMUNICATION

After you have informed the executive, you must quickly update the company and your staff on the change. The correct order for informing the company is (1) the executive's direct reports—because they will be most impacted; (2) the other members of your staff—because they will need to answer questions about it; and (3) the rest of the company. All of these communications should happen on the same day and preferably within a couple of hours. When disclosing the firing to the direct reports, make sure that you have a plan for whom they will report to in the meantime and what's next (executive search, reorganization, internal promotion, or something else). Generally, it's smart for the CEO to act in the executive role in the meanwhile. If you do act in the role, you must really act—staff meetings, one-on-ones, objective setting, etc. Doing so will provide excellent continuity for the team and greatly inform your thinking on whom to hire next.

As you did when you updated the board, keep the message positive and refrain from throwing the executive under the bus. The best employees in the organization will likely be the ones closest to the executive. If you trash her, you will put all her best employees on notice that they are next. Is that a message you want to send?

When you update the company, you might worry about employees misinterpreting the news and thinking the company is in trouble. Do not try to maneuver around such a reaction. When you expect your employees to act like adults, they generally do. If you treat them like children, then get ready for your company to turn into one big *Barney* episode.

## IN THE END

Every CEO likes to say she runs a great company. It's hard to tell whether the claim is true until the company or the CEO has to do something really difficult. Firing an executive is a good test.

# DEMOTING A LOYAL FRIEND

When I started Loudcloud, I hired the best people I knew—people whom I respected, trusted, and liked. Like me, many of them did not have deep experience in the jobs that I gave them, but they worked night and day to learn, and they made great contributions to the company. Nevertheless, the day came when I needed to hire someone else, someone with more experience, to run the function that I had previously entrusted to my loyal friend. Damn. How do you do that?

## SHOULD YOU DO IT AT ALL?

The first question that always comes to mind is "Do I really need to do this? Who could I possibly hire who will work this hard and bleed the company colors like this?" Sadly, if you're asking the question, you very likely already know the answer. If you need to build a worldwide sales organization, your buddy who did the first few deals is almost certainly not the best choice. As hard as it may be, you need to take a Confucian approach. You must consider first all of the other employees and second your friend. The good of the individual must be sacrificed for the good of the whole.

## HOW DO YOU BREAK THE NEWS?

Once you make the decision, breaking the news will not be easy. It's important to consider two deep emotions your friend will feel:

- **Embarrassment** Do not underestimate what a large factor this will be in his thinking. All of his friends, relatives, and colleagues know his current position. They know how hard he's worked and how much he's sacrificed for the company. How will he possibly explain to them that he will no longer be part of the executive team?

- **Betrayal** Your friend will undoubtedly feel something like this: I've been there from the beginning, I've worked side by side with you. How could you do this? It's not like you're perfect in your job, either. How can you be so comfortable selling me out?

Those are some powerful emotions, so get ready for an intense discussion. Ironically, the key to an emotional discussion is to take the emotion out of it. To do that, you must be very clear in your mind about what you've decided and what you want to do.

The most important thing to decide is that you really want to do this. If you walk into a demotion discussion with an open decision, you will walk out with a mess: a mess of a situation and a mess of a relationship. As part of the decision, you must get comfortable with the thought that the employee may quit the company. Given the intense emotions he will feel, there is no guarantee that he will want to stay. If you cannot afford to lose him, you cannot make this change.

Finally, you must decide the best role for him in your company. The obvious thing is to have him continue under his new boss, but this may not be the best thing for him, his boss, or his career. Your loyal employee will continue to have lots of knowledge about your company, competition, customers, and market that his new boss lacks.

On the one hand, this can be a good thing—he can help get the new boss up to speed. On the other hand, when mixed with the intense emotions of embarrassment and betrayal, you might end up with a sabotage cocktail.

Another problem with this approach is that from a career path perspective there is no way to paint a picture of him reporting to his new boss as anything but a demotion. An alternative, if appropriate, would be to move him to another area of the company where his skills, talent, and knowledge will help. This kind of move will give him a chance to develop a new set of skills and help the company while he's doing it. For young employees, getting experience in different areas can be highly valuable.

Sadly, this option may not be a silver bullet. He might not want to work in another job; he might be hell-bent on keeping his current job, so prepare for that as well.

Once you've decided to hire someone above your friend and decided on the alternatives that you'd like to offer him, you can have the conversation. Keep in mind that you cannot let him keep his old job, but you can be fair and you can be honest. Some keys to doing that:

- *Use appropriate language.* Make clear with your language that you've decided. As previously discussed, use phrases like "I have decided" rather than "I think" or "I'd like." By doing this, you will avoid putting the employee in the awkward position of wondering whether he should lobby for his old job. You can't tell him what he wants to hear, but you can be honest.

- *Admit reality.* If you are a founder-CEO like I was, it probably won't be lost on the employee that you are just as underskilled for your job as he is for his. Don't dodge this fact. In fact, admit that if you were a more experienced CEO, you might be able to develop him into the role, but two people who don't know what they are doing is a recipe for failure.

- *Acknowledge the contributions.* If you want him to stay in the company, you should say that and make it crystal clear that you want to help him develop his career and contribute to the company. Let him know that you appreciate what he's done and that your decision results from a forward-looking examination of what the company needs, not a review of his past performance. The best way to do this, if appropriate, is to couple the demotion with an *increase* in compensation. Doing so will let him know that he's both appreciated and valued going forward.

Through all of this, keep in mind that it is what it is and nothing you can say will change that or stop it from being deeply upsetting. Your goal should not be to take the sting out of it, but to be honest, clear, and effective. Your friend may not appreciate that in the moment, but he will appreciate it over time.

# LIES THAT LOSERS TELL

When a company starts to lose its major battles, the truth often becomes the first casualty. CEOs and employees work tirelessly to develop creative narratives that help them avoid dealing with the obvious facts. Despite their intense creativity, many companies often end up with the same false explanations.

## SOME FAMILIAR LIES

"She left, but we were going to fire her, or give her a bad performance review." High-tech companies tend to track employee attrition in three categories:

1. People who quit

2. People who got fired

3. People who quit, but it's okay because the company didn't want them anyway

Fascinatingly, as companies begin to struggle, the third category always seems to grow much faster than the first. In addition, the sudden wave of "semi-performance-related attrition" usually happens in companies that claim to have a "super-high talent bar." How do all these superstar employees suddenly go from great to crap? How is it possible that when you lose a top-rated employee before you can say "unwanted attrition," the manager carefully explains how her performance fell off?

"We would have won, but the other guys gave the deal away." "The customer selected us technically and thinks we are the better company, but our competitor just gave the product away. We would never sell so cheaply as it would hurt our reputation." Anybody who has ever run an enterprise sales force has heard this lie before. You go into an account, you fight hard, and you lose. The sales rep, not wanting to shine the light on himself, blames the "used car dealer" rep from the other company. The CEO, not wanting to believe that she's losing product competitiveness, believes the rep. If you hear this lie, try to validate the claim with the actual customer. I'll bet you can't.

"Just because we missed the intermediate milestones doesn't mean we won't hit our product schedule." In engineering meetings where there is great pressure to ship on time—a customer commitment, a quarter that depends on it, or a competitive imperative—everybody hopes for good news. When the facts don't align with the good news, a clever manager will find the narrative to make everybody feel better— until the next meeting.

"We have a very high churn rate, but as soon as we turn on email marketing to our user base, people will come back." Yes, of course. The reason that people leave our service and don't come back is that we have not been sending them enough spam. That makes total sense to me, too.

Where do lies come from?

To answer that question, I thought back to a conversation I had years ago with the incomparable Andy Grove.

Back at the tail end of the Great Internet Bubble in 2001, as all the big technology companies began missing their quarters by giant amounts, I found myself wondering how none of them saw it coming.

One would think that after the dot-com crash of April 2000, companies like Cisco, Siebel, and HP would realize that they would soon face a slowdown as many of their customers hit the wall. But despite perhaps the most massive and public early warning system ever, each CEO reiterated strong guidance right up to the point where they dramatically whiffed their quarters.

I asked Andy why these great CEOs would lie about their impending fate.

He said they were not lying to investors, but rather, they were lying to themselves.

Andy explained that humans, particularly those who build things, only listen to leading indicators of good news. For example, if a CEO hears that engagement for her application increased an incremental 25 percent beyond the normal growth rate one month, she will be off to the races hiring more engineers to keep up with the impending tidal wave of demand. On the other hand, if engagement decreases 25 percent, she will be equally intense and urgent in explaining it away: "The site was slow that month, there were four holidays, and we made a UI change that caused all the problems. For gosh sakes, let's not panic!"

Both leading indicators may have been wrong, or both may have been right, but our hypothetical CEO—like almost every other CEO—only took action on the positive indicator and only looked for alternative explanations on the negative leading indicator.

If this advice sounds too familiar. and you find yourself wondering why your honest employees are lying to you, the answer is they are not. They are lying to themselves.

And if you believe them, you are lying to yourself.

# LEAD BULLETS

Early in my tenure at Netscape, when we realized that Microsoft's new Web server had every feature that ours had, but was also five times faster and was to be given away for free, I immediately went to work trying to pivot our server product line to something that we could sell for money. The late, great Mike Homer and I worked furiously on a set of partnerships and acquisitions that would broaden the product line and surround the Web server with enough functionality that we would be able to survive the attack.

I excitedly reviewed the plan with my engineering counterpart, Bill Turpin, who looked at me as though I were a little kid who had much to learn. Bill was a longtime veteran of battling Microsoft from his time at Borland and understood what I was trying to do, but he was not persuaded. He said, "Ben, those silver bullets that you and Mike are looking for are fine and good, but our Web server is five times slower. There is no silver bullet that's going to fix that. No, we are going to have to use a lot of lead bullets." Oh snap.

As a result of Bill's advice, we focused our engineering team on fixing the performance issues while working on the other things in the background. We eventually beat Microsoft's performance and grew the server line to become a $400 million business, and we would never have done it without those lead bullets.

I carried that lesson with me for many years. Six years later, when I was CEO of Opsware, our toughest competitor, BladeLogic, started to consistently beat us in large deals. We were a public company, and the losses were all too visible. To make matters worse, we needed to win those deals in order to beat Wall Street's projections, so the company felt tremendous pressure. Many of our smartest people came to me with ideas for avoiding the battle:

- "Let's build a lightweight version of the product and go down-market."

- "Let's acquire a company with a simpler architecture."

- "Let's focus on service providers."

All these approaches reinforced to me was that we weren't facing a market problem. The customers were buying; they just weren't buying *our* product. This was not a time to pivot. So I said the same thing to every one of them: "There are no silver bullets for this, only lead bullets." They did not want to hear that, but it made things clear: We had to build a better product. There was no other way out. No window, no hole, no escape hatch, no back door. We had to go through the front door and deal with the big, ugly guy blocking it. Lead bullets.

After nine months of hard work on an extremely rugged product cycle, we regained our product lead and eventually built a company that was worth $1.6 billion. Without the lead bullets, I suspect we would have ended at about one-tenth that value.

There may be nothing scarier in business than facing an existential threat. So scary that many in the organization will do anything to avoid facing it. They will look for any alternative, any way out, any excuse not to live or die in a single battle. I see this often in startup pitches. The conversations go something like this:

Entrepreneur: "We have the best product in the market by far. All the customers love it and prefer it to competitor X."

Me: "Why does competitor X have five times your revenue?"

Entrepreneur: "We are using partners and OEMs, because we can't build a direct channel like competitor X."

Me: "Why not? If you have the better product, why not knuckle up and go to war?"

Entrepreneur: "Ummm."

Me: "Stop looking for the silver bullet."

There comes a time in every company's life where it must fight for its life. If you find yourself running when you should be fighting, you need to ask yourself, "If our company isn't good enough to win, then do we need to exist at all?"

# NOBODY CARES

"Just win, baby."

—AL DAVIS

Back in those bad old days at Loudcloud, I often thought to myself: How could I have possibly prepared for this? How could I know that half our customers would go out of business? How could I know that it would become impossible to raise money in the private markets? How could I have figured out that there would be 221 IPOs in 2000 and 19 in 2001? Could anybody expect me to achieve a reasonable outcome given those circumstances?

As I was feeling sorry for myself, I randomly watched an interview with famous football coach Bill Parcells. He was telling the story of how he had a similar dilemma when he began his head coaching career. In his very first season, Parcells's team, the New York Giants, was hit with a rash of injuries. He worried incessantly about the impact of the injuries on his team's fortunes, as it is difficult enough to win with your best players, let alone a bunch of substitutes. When his friend and mentor, Raiders owner Al Davis, called Parcells to check in, Parcells relayed his injury issues.

Parcells: "Al, I am just not sure how we can win without so many of our best players. What should I do?"

Davis: "Bill, nobody cares, just coach your team."

That might be the best CEO advice ever. Because, you see, nobody cares. When things go wrong in your company, nobody cares. The media don't care, your investors don't care, your board doesn't care, your employees don't care, and even your mama doesn't care.

Nobody cares.

And they are right not to care. A great reason for failing won't preserve one dollar for your investors, won't save one employee's job, or get you one new customer. It especially won't make you feel one bit better when you shut down your company and declare bankruptcy.

All the mental energy you use to elaborate your misery would be far better used trying to find the one seemingly impossible way out of your current mess. Spend zero time on what you could have done, and devote all of your time on what you might do. Because in the end, nobody cares; just run your company.

# CHAPTER 5

# TAKE CARE OF THE PEOPLE, THE PRODUCTS, AND THE PROFITS— IN THAT ORDER

"I roll with the hardest niggas, make money with the smartest niggas
I ain't got time for you fuckin artist niggas
Better shut your trap before you become a target nigga
Y'all army brats I'm the motherfuckin sergeant nigga."
—THE GAME, "SCREAM ON 'EM"

Once we pushed the Opsware stock price back above $1, the next problem was to rebuild the executive team. We had cloud services executives, but now we were a software company and needed software executives. In enterprise software companies, the two most important positions tend to be VP of sales and VP of engineering. Initially I'd attempted to take the VP of professional services from Loudcloud and make him the VP of sales. That didn't work. The next head of sales would be the fourth one hired since we had founded the company three years earlier—not a great track record. More important, the next mistake I made on a sales leader would be my last. The marketplace, not to mention Wall Street investors, did not leave me with much rope.

To better prepare for the hire this time, I decided in the interim to run sales myself. I managed the team, ran the forecast calls, and was the one person responsible for the revenue number for Opsware. I'd learned the hard way that when hiring executives, one should follow Colin Powell's instructions and hire for strength rather than lack of weakness. By running sales, I understood very clearly the strengths we needed. I made a careful list and set out to find the sales executives with the right skills and talents for Opsware.

After interviewing about two dozen candidates—none of whom had the strengths I sought—I interviewed Mark Cranney. He wasn't what I expected; he didn't fit the stereotype of a hard-charging sales executive. For starters, Mark was average height, whereas most sales executives tend to be rather tall. Next, he was a square guy—that is, he was as wide as he was tall. Not fat, just square. His square body seemed to fit rather uncomfortably into what must have been a custom-tailored suit—there is no way an off-the-rack business suit would fit a square guy like Mark.

And then I looked at his résumé. The first thing I noticed was that he went to a school that I'd never heard of, Southern Utah University. I asked him what kind of school it was. He replied, "It was the MIT of southern Utah." That was the last joke he told. Mark's seriousness was so intense that it seemed to make him uncomfortable in his own skin. He made me uncomfortable, too. Ordinarily, that vibe would rule out a candidate for me, but the strengths that I needed were so critical to the business that I was willing to overlook every weakness. One interview technique that I'd used to sort the good from the bad was to ask a series of questions about hiring, training, and managing sales reps. Typically, it would go like this:

Ben: "What do you look for in a sales rep?"

Candidate: "They need to be smart, aggressive, and competitive. They need to know how to do complex deals and navigate organizations."

Ben: "How do you test for those things in an interview?"

Candidate: "Umm, well, I hire everybody out of my network."

Ben: "Okay, once you get them on board, what do you expect from them?"

Candidate: "I expect them to understand and follow the sales process, I expect them to master the product, I expect them to be accurate in their forecasting. . . ."

Ben: "Tell me about the training program that you designed to achieve this."

Candidate: "Umm." They would then proceed to make something up as they went along.

Mark aced the profile and interview questions, and then I asked him the training question. I'll never forget the pained look that came across his face. He looked like he wanted to get up and leave the interview right then and there. I felt like offering him an aspirin or maybe some Abilify. His reaction surprised me, because he'd done such an excellent job up to that point. I later realized that for me to ask Mark Cranney to describe the proper way to train sales reps was like a layman asking Isaac Newton to explain the laws of physics. Where to begin?

After what seemed like five minutes of silence, Mark reached into his bag and pulled out a giant training manual he had designed. He said he couldn't possibly explain what I needed to know about training in the time we had left, but if I wanted to schedule a follow-up meeting, he would explain the nuances of training sales people to be elite across a broad set of disciplines including process, products, and organizational selling. He explained further that even with all those things, a successful sales leader still must inspire courage in the team. He sounded like General Patton. I knew I had my guy.

Unfortunately, nobody else knew that. Every member of the executive staff (with one exception) and every member of the board of directors voted thumbs-down on Mark Cranney. When I asked Bill Campbell what he thought, he said, "I won't lay down on the railroad tracks to stop you from hiring Cranney." That wasn't the ringing endorsement I was looking for. The reasons for voting "no" never referred to Mark's lack of strength, but rather to his abundance of weakness: Mark went to Southern Utah. Mark made people feel uncomfortable. Mark did not look like a head of sales.

Still, the more time I spent with him, the more I knew he was the one. In talking with him for an hour, I'd learn more about sales than I had in six months running sales. He would even call me with details about deals my sales team was competing for—deals my own sales reps didn't seem to know about. It was like he had his own sales FBI.

I decided to take a stand. I told my team and the board that I understood their concerns, but I still wanted to move forward with Mark and planned to proceed with reference checks.

When I asked Mark for his references, he surprised me again. He gave me a list of seventy-five references. He said he had more if I needed them. I called every reference on the list, and every one called me back within one hour. Mark ran a tight network. Maybe these references were the sales FBI. Then, just as I was getting ready to make the hire, another executive on my team called to say that a friend of hers knew Mark Cranney and wanted to give a negative reference.

I called the friend—I'll call him Joe—and proceeded to have the most unusual reference call of my career:

Ben: "Thanks very much for reaching out."

Joe: "My pleasure."

Ben: "How do you know Mark Cranney?"

Joe: "Mark was an area vice president when I taught sales training at my previous employer. I want to tell you that under no circumstances should you hire Mark Cranney."

Ben: "Wow, that's a strong statement. Is he a criminal?"

Joe: "No, I've never known Mark to do anything unethical."

Ben: "Is he bad at hiring?"

Joe: "No, he brought some of the best salespeople into the company."

Ben: "Can he do big deals?"

Joe: "Yes, definitely. Mark did some of the largest deals we had."

Ben: "Is he a bad manager?"

Joe: "No, he was very effective at running his team."

Ben: "Well, then why shouldn't I hire him?"

Joe: "He'll be a terrible cultural fit."

Ben: "Please explain."

Joe: "Well, when I was teaching new-hire sales training at Parametric Technology Corporation, I brought in Mark as a guest speaker to fire up the troops. We had fifty new hires and I had them all excited about selling and enthusiastic about working for the company. Mark Cranney walks up to the podium, looks at the crowd of fresh new recruits, and says, 'I don't give a fuck how well trained you are. If you don't bring me five hundred thousand dollars a quarter, I'm putting a bullet in your head.'"

Ben: "Thank you very much."

The world looks one way in peacetime but very different when you must fight for your life every day. In times of peace, one has time to care about things like appropriateness, long-term cultural consequences, and people's feelings. In times of war, killing the enemy and getting the troops safely home is all that counts. I was at war and I needed a wartime general. I needed Mark Cranney.

As a final step in making the hire, I needed to explain it to Marc Andreessen. As cofounder and chairman of the board, Marc's opinion mattered deeply to the board and Marc was still uncomfortable with Cranney. Marc trusted me enough that he would let me make the hire whether he liked the candidate or not, but it was important to me that Marc be fully on board.

I let Marc open the conversation, because despite consistently being the smartest person in the room and possibly the world, Marc is so humble that he never believes that other people think he is smart, which makes him sensitive to being ignored. He opened the conversation by listing his issues with Cranney: doesn't look or sound like a head of sales, went to a weak school, makes him uncomfortable. I listened very carefully and replied, "I agree with every single one of those issues. However, Mark Cranney is a sales savant. He has mastered sales to a level that far exceeds anybody that I have ever known. If he didn't have the things wrong with him that you enumerated, he wouldn't be willing to join a company that just traded at thirty-five cents per share; he'd be CEO of IBM."

Marc's reply came quickly: "Got it. Let's hire him!"

And that's how I took the key step in building a world-class software team out of the Loudcloud rubble. As I got to know Mark over the years, everything that I learned in the interview and the reference check proved out. He wasn't an easy cultural fit, but he was a genius. I needed his genius and worked with him on the fit. I don't know that every member of the team ever became totally comfortable with Mark, but in the end they all agreed that he was the best person possible for the job.


My old boss Jim Barksdale was fond of saying, "We take care of the people, the products, and the profits—in that order." It's a simple saying, but it's deep. "Taking care of the people" is the most difficult of the three by far and if you don't do it, the other two won't matter. Taking care of the people means that your company is a good place to work. Most workplaces are far from good. As organizations grow large, important work can go unnoticed, the hardest workers can get passed over by the best politicians, and bureaucratic processes can choke out the creativity and remove all the joy.

When everything went wrong from the dot-com crash to NASDAQ threatening to delist the company, the thing that saved us were the techniques developed in this chapter. If your company is a good place to work, you too may live long enough to find your glory.

# A GOOD PLACE TO WORK

At Opsware I used to teach a management expectations course because I deeply believed in training. I made it clear that I expected every manager to meet with her people on a regular basis. I even gave instructions on how to conduct a one-on-one meeting so there could be no excuses.

Then one day, while I happily went about my job, it came to my attention that one of my managers hadn't had a one-on-one meeting with any of his employees in more than six months. While I knew to "expect what I inspect," I did not expect this. No one-on-one in more than six months? How was it possible for me to invest so much time thinking about management, preparing materials, and personally training my managers and then get no one-on-ones for six months? Wow, so much for CEO authority. If that's how the managers listen to me, then why do I even bother coming to work?

I thought that leading by example would be the sure way to get the company to do what I wanted. Lord knows the company picked up all of my bad habits, so why didn't they pick up my good habits? Had I lost the team? I recalled a conversation I'd had with my father many years ago regarding Tommy Heinsohn, the Boston Celtics basketball coach at the time. Heinsohn had been one of the most successful coaches in the world, including being named coach of the year and winning two NBA championships.

However, he had gone downhill fast and now had the worst record in the league. I asked my father what happened. He said, "The players stopped paying attention to his temper tantrums. Heinsohn used to yell at the team and they'd respond. Now they just ignore him." Was the team now ignoring me? Had I yelled at them one time too many?

The more I thought about it, the more I realized that while I had told the team "what" to do, I had not been clear about "why" I wanted them to do it. Clearly, my authority alone was not enough to get them to do what I wanted. Given the large number of things that we were trying to accomplish, managers couldn't get to everything and came up with their own priorities. Apparently, this manager didn't think that meeting with his people was all that important and I hadn't explained to him why it was so important.

So why did I force every manager through management training? Why did I demand that managers have one-on-ones with employees? After much deliberation with myself, I settled on an articulation of the core reason and I called up the offending manager's boss—I'll call him Steve—and told him that I needed to see him right away.

When Steve came into my office I asked him a question: "Steve, do you know why I came to work today?"

Steve: "What do you mean, Ben?"

Me: "Why did I bother waking up? Why did I bother coming in? If it was about the money, couldn't I sell the company tomorrow and have more money than I ever wanted? I don't want to be famous, in fact just the opposite."

Steve: "I guess."

Me: "Well, then why did I come to work?"

Steve: "I don't know."

Me: "Well, let me explain. I came to work because it's personally very important to me that Opsware be a good company. It's important to me that the people who spend twelve to sixteen hours a day here, which is most of their waking life, have a good life. It's why I come to work."

Steve: "Okay."

Me: "Do you know the difference between a good place to work and a bad place to work?"

Steve: "Umm, I think so."

Me: "What is the difference?"

Steve: "Umm, well . . ."

Me: "Let me break it down for you. In good organizations, people can focus on their work and have confidence that if they get their work done, good things will happen for both the company and them personally. It is a true pleasure to work in an organization such as this. Every person can wake up knowing that the work they do will be efficient, effective, and make a difference for the organization and themselves. These things make their jobs both motivating and fulfilling.

"In a poor organization, on the other hand, people spend much of their time fighting organizational boundaries, infighting, and broken processes. They are not even clear on what their jobs are, so there is no way to know if they are getting the job done or not. In the miracle case that they work ridiculous hours and get the job done, they have no idea what it means for the company or their careers. To make it all much worse and rub salt in the wound, when they finally work up the courage to tell management how fucked-up their situation is, management denies there is a problem, then defends the status quo, then ignores the problem."

Steve: "Okay."

Me: "Are you aware that your manager Tim has not met with any of his employees in the past six months?"

Steve: "No."

Me: "Now that you are aware, do you realize that there is no possible way for him to even be informed as to whether or not his organization is good or bad?"

Steve: "Yes."

Me: "In summary, you and Tim are preventing me from achieving my one and only goal. You have become a barrier blocking me from achieving my most important goal. As a result, if Tim doesn't meet with each one of his employees in the next twenty-four hours, I will have no choice but to fire him and to fire you. Are we clear?"

Steve: "Crystal."

## WAS THAT REALLY NECESSARY?

You might argue that no matter how well managed a company is, it will fail without product/market fit. You might argue further that horribly managed companies that achieve massive product/market fit succeed just fine. And you would be right on both accounts. So was it really necessary for me to make such a dramatic speech and threaten one of my executives?

I think it was, for the following three reasons:

- Being a good company doesn't matter when things go well, but it can be the difference between life and death when things go wrong.

- Things always go wrong.

- Being a good company is an end in itself.

## THE DIFFERENCE BETWEEN LIFE AND DEATH

When things go well, the reasons to stay at a company are many:

- Your career path is wide open because as the company grows lots of interesting jobs naturally open up.

- Your friends and family think you are a genius for choosing to work at the "it" company before anyone else knew it was "it."

- Your résumé gets stronger by working at a blue-chip company in its heyday.

- Oh, and you are getting rich.

When things go poorly, all those reasons become reasons to leave. In fact, the only thing that keeps an employee at a company when things go horribly wrong—other than needing a job—is that she likes her job.

## THINGS ALWAYS GO WRONG

There has never been a company in the history of the world that had a monotonically increasing stock price. In bad companies, when the economics disappear, so do the employees. In technology companies, when the employees disappear, the spiral begins: The company declines in value, the best employees leave, the company declines in value, the best employees leave. Spirals are extremely difficult to reverse.

## BEING A GOOD COMPANY
## IS AN END IN ITSELF

When I first met Bill Campbell, he was chairman of Intuit, on the board of Apple, and a mentor to many of the top CEOs in the industry. However, those things did not impress me nearly as much as his time running GO Corporation back in 1992. The company raised more money than almost any other venture-capital-backed startup in history and lost nearly all of it before selling itself for nearly nothing to AT&T in 1994.

Now that probably doesn't sound impressive. In fact, it probably sounds like a horrible failure. But I'd met dozens of GO employees in my career, including great people like Mike Homer, Danny Shader,

Frank Chen, and Stratton Sclavos. The amazing thing was that every one of those GO employees counted GO as one of the greatest work experiences of their lives. The best work experience ever despite the fact that their careers stood still, they made no money, and they were front-page failures. GO was a good place to work.

This made me realize what an amazingly effective CEO Bill was. Apparently, John Doerr thought that, too, because when Scott Cook needed a CEO for Intuit, John recommended Bill even though Bill lost a ton of John's money at GO. And for years, everyone who ever came into contact with GO employees knew what Bill was about. He was about building good companies.

If you do nothing else, be like Bill and build a good company.

# WHY STARTUPS SHOULD
# TRAIN THEIR PEOPLE

I learned about why startups should train their people when I worked at Netscape. People at McDonald's get trained for their positions, but people with far more complicated jobs don't. It makes no sense. Would you want to stand on the line of the untrained person at McDonald's? Would you want to use the software written by the engineer who was never told how the rest of the code worked? A lot of companies think their employees are so smart that they require no training. That's silly.

When I first became a manager, I had mixed feelings about training. Logically, training for high-tech companies made sense, but my personal experience with training programs at the companies where I had worked was underwhelming. The courses were taught by outside firms who didn't really understand our business and were teaching things that weren't relevant. Then I read chapter 16 of Andy Grove's management classic, *High Output Management*, titled "Why Training Is the Boss's Job," and it changed my career. Grove wrote, "Most managers seem to feel that training employees is a job that should be left to others. I, on the other hand, strongly believe that the manager should do it himself."

When I was director of product management at Netscape, I was feeling frustrated by how little value most product managers added to the business. Based on Andy's guidance, I wrote a short document called "Good Product Manager/Bad Product Manager," which I used to train the team on my basic expectations. (That document follows on page 111.) I was shocked by what happened next. The performance of my team instantly improved. Product managers whom I had almost written off as hopeless became effective. Pretty soon I was managing the highest-performing team in the company. Based on this experience, after starting Loudcloud, I heavily invested in training. I credit that investment with much of our eventual success. And the whole thing started with a simple decision to train my people and an even simpler training document. So, I will now pay forward my debt to Andy Grove and explain why, what, and how you should do the same in your company.

## WHY YOU SHOULD TRAIN YOUR PEOPLE

Almost everyone who builds a technology company knows that people are the most important asset. Properly run startups place a great deal of emphasis on recruiting and the interview process in order to build their talent base. Too often the investment in people stops there. There are four core reasons why it shouldn't:

### 1. Productivity

I often see startups keep careful statistics of how many candidates they've screened, how many have made it to the full interview process, and how many people they've hired. All of these statistics are interesting, but the most important statistic is missing: How many fully productive employees have they added? By failing to measure progress toward the actual goal, they lose sight of the value of training. If they measured productivity, they might be horrified to find that all those investments in recruiting, hiring, and integration were going to waste. Even if they were made aware of low productivity among new employees, most

CEOs think that they don't have time to invest in training. Andy Grove does the math and shows that the opposite is true:

> *Training is, quite simply, one of the highest-leverage activities a manager can perform. Consider for a moment the possibility of your putting on a series of four lectures for members of your department. Let's count on three hours preparation for each hour of course time—twelve hours of work in total. Say that you have ten students in your class.*
>
> *Next year they will work a total of about twenty thousand hours for your organization. If your training efforts result in a 1 percent improvement in your subordinates' performance, your company will gain the equivalent of two hundred hours of work as the result of the expenditure of your twelve hours.*

## 2. Performance management

When people interview managers, they often like to ask, Have you fired anyone? Or how many people have you fired? Or how would you go about firing someone? These are all fine questions, but often the right question is the one that isn't asked: When you fired the person, how did you know with certainty that the employee both understood the expectations of the job and was still missing them? The best answer is that the manager clearly set expectations when she trained the employee for the job. If you don't train your people, you establish no basis for performance management. As a result, performance management in your company will be sloppy and inconsistent.

## 3. Product quality

Often founders start companies with visions of elegant, beautiful product architectures that will solve so many of the nasty issues that they were forced to deal with in their previous jobs. Then, as their company becomes successful, they find that their beautiful product architecture has turned into a Frankenstein. How does this happen? As success drives the need to hire new engineers at a rapid rate, companies neglect to train the new engineers properly. As the engineers are assigned tasks, they figure out how to complete them as best they can. Often this means replicating existing facilities in the architecture, which leads to inconsistencies in the user experience, performance problems, and a general mess. And you thought training was expensive.

### 4. Employee retention

During a time of particularly high attrition at Netscape, I decided to read all of the exit interviews for the entire company to better understand why people quit high-tech companies. After putting economics aside, I found that there were two primary reasons why people quit:

- They hated their manager; generally the employees were appalled by the lack of guidance, career development, and feedback they were receiving.

- They weren't learning anything: The company wasn't investing resources in helping employees develop new skills.

An outstanding training program can address both issues head-on.

### WHAT SHOULD YOU DO FIRST?

The best place to start is with the topic that is most relevant to your employees: the knowledge and skill that they need to do their job. I call this functional training. Functional training can be as simple as training a new employee on your expectations for them (see "Good Product Manager/Bad Product Manager") and as complex as a multiweek engineering boot camp to bring new recruits completely up to speed on all of the historical architectural nuances of your product. The training courses should be tailored to the specific job. If you attempt the more complex-style course, be sure to enlist the best experts on the team as well as the manager. As a happy side effect, this type of effort will do more to build a powerful, positive company culture than a hundred culture-building strategic off-site meetings.

The other essential component of a company's training program is management training. Management training is the best place to start setting expectations for your management team. Do you expect them to hold regular one-on-one meetings with their employees? Do you expect them to give performance feedback? Do you expect them to train their people? Do you expect them to agree on objectives with their team? If you do, then you'd better tell them, because the management state of the art in technology companies is extremely poor. Once you've set expectations, the next set of management courses has already been defined; they are the courses that teach your managers how to do the things you expect (how to write a performance review or how to conduct a one-on-one).

Once you have management training and functional training in place, there are other opportunities as well. One of the great things about building a tech company is the amazing people that you can hire. Take your best people and encourage them to share their most developed skills. Training in such topics as negotiating, interviewing, and finance will enhance your company's competency in those areas as well as improve employee morale. Teaching can also become a badge of honor for employees who achieve an elite level of competence.

## IMPLEMENTING YOUR TRAINING PROGRAM

Now that we understand the value of the training and what to train on, how do we get our organization to do what we want? The first thing to recognize is that no startup has time to do optional things. Therefore, training must be mandatory. The first two types of training (functional and management) can be easily enforced as follows:

- Enforce functional training by withholding new employee requisitions. As Andy Grove writes, there are only two ways for a manager to improve the output of an employee: motivation and training. Therefore, training should be the most basic requirement for all managers in your organization. An effective way to enforce this requirement is by withholding new employee requisitions from managers until they've developed a training program for the TBH, "To Be Hired."

- Enforce management training by teaching it yourself. Managing the company is the CEO's job. While you won't have time to teach all of the management courses yourself, you should teach the course on management expectations, because they are, after all, *your* expectations. Make it an honor to participate in these sessions by selecting the best managers on your team to teach the other courses. And make that mandatory, too.

Ironically, the biggest obstacle to putting a training program in place is the perception that it will take too much time. Keep in mind that there is no investment that you can make that will do more to improve productivity in your company. Therefore, being too busy to train is the moral equivalent of being too hungry to eat. Furthermore, it's not that hard to create basic training courses.

When I ran the server product management group at Netscape, I became extremely frustrated that everybody on the team I inherited had a completely unique and different interpretation of their job. Finally, I had an epiphany that nobody in the industry had ever defined the product management job. What follows was my attempt to do that and bring down my blood pressure. Amazingly, people still read it today. This taught me the importance of training.

## GOOD PRODUCT MANAGER/ BAD PRODUCT MANAGER

Good product managers know the market, the product, the product line, and the competition extremely well and operate from a strong basis of knowledge and confidence. A good product manager is the CEO of the product. Good product managers take full responsibility and measure themselves in terms of the success of the product.

They are responsible for right product/right time and all that entails. A good product manager knows the context going in (the company, our revenue funding, competition, etc.), and they take responsibility for devising and executing a winning plan (no excuses).

Bad product managers have lots of excuses. Not enough funding, the engineering manager is an idiot, Microsoft has ten times as many engineers working on it, I'm overworked, I don't get enough direction. Our CEO doesn't make these kinds of excuses and neither should the CEO of a product.

Good product managers don't get all of their time sucked up by the various organizations that must work together to deliver the right product at the right time. They don't take all the product team minutes; they don't project manage the various functions; they are not gofers for engineering. They are not part of the product team; they manage the product team. Engineering teams don't consider good product managers a "marketing resource." Good product managers are the marketing counterparts to the engineering manager.

Good product managers crisply define the target, the "what" (as opposed to the "how"), and manage the delivery of the "what." Bad product managers feel best about themselves when they figure out "how." Good product managers communicate crisply to engineering in writing as well as verbally. Good product managers don't give direction informally. Good product managers gather information informally.

Good product managers create collateral, FAQs, presentations, and white papers that can be leveraged by salespeople, marketing people, and executives. Bad product managers complain that they spend all day answering questions for the sales force and are swamped. Good product managers anticipate the serious product flaws and build real solutions. Bad product managers put out fires all day.

Good product managers take written positions on important issues (competitive silver bullets, tough architectural choices, tough product decisions, and markets to attack or yield). Bad product managers voice their opinions verbally and lament that the "powers that be" won't let it happen. Once bad product managers fail, they point out that they predicted they would fail.

Good product managers focus the team on revenue and customers. Bad product managers focus the team on how many features competitors are building. Good product managers define good products that can be executed with a strong effort. Bad product managers define good products that can't be executed or let engineering build whatever they want (that is, solve the hardest problem).

Good product managers think in terms of delivering superior value to the marketplace during product planning and achieving market share and revenue goals during the go-to-market phase. Bad product managers get very confused about the differences among delivering value, matching competitive features, pricing, and ubiquity. Good product managers decompose problems. Bad product managers combine all problems into one.

Good product managers think about the story they want written by the press. Bad product managers think about covering every feature and being absolutely technically accurate with the press. Good product managers ask the press questions. Bad product managers answer any press question. Good product managers assume members of the press and the analyst community are really smart. Bad product managers assume that journalists and analysts are dumb because they don't understand the subtle nuances of their particular technology.

Good product managers err on the side of clarity. Bad product managers never even explain the obvious. Good product managers define their job and their success. Bad product managers constantly want to be told what to do.

Good product managers send their status reports in on time every week, because they are disciplined. Bad product managers forget to send in their status reports on time, because they don't value discipline.

# IS IT OKAY TO HIRE PEOPLE FROM YOUR FRIEND'S COMPANY?

Every good technology company needs great people. The best companies invest time, money, and sweat equity into becoming world-class recruiting machines. But how far should you take your quest to build the world's greatest team? Is it fair game to hire employees from your friend's company? Will you still be friends?

First, what do I mean by "friends"? There are two relevant categories:

- Important business partners

- Friends

For this discussion, friends and important business partners are roughly the same.

Most CEOs would never target a friend's company as a source of talent. As CEO, one generally doesn't have many true friends in business, and raiding your friend's company is a sure way to lose one. Nevertheless, almost every CEO will be faced with the decision of whether to hire an employee out of her friend's company. How does it happen? When is it okay? When will it cost you a friend?

## BUT THEY WERE ALREADY LOOKING

It always starts in the same way. Your friend Cathy has a great engineer working for her named Mitchell. Mitchell happens to be friends with one of your top engineers. Your engineer brings Mitchell in for an interview, unbeknownst to you, and he naturally sails through the process. The final step is the interview with you, the CEO. You immediately notice that Mitchell currently works at your good friend Cathy's company. You check with your people to make sure that they did not approach Mitchell first, and they assure you that Mitchell was already looking and will go to another company if not yours. Now what?

At this point, you might be thinking, "If Mitchell is leaving, then logically my friend Cathy should want him to go to my company rather than to a competitor or a company with a CEO whom she doesn't like." Maybe Cathy will see it that way, but probably not.

People generally leave companies when things are not going well, so you should assume that Cathy is fighting for her company's life. In this situation, nothing will cut her deeper than losing a great employee, because she knows that the other employees will see that as a leading indicator of the company's demise. Even more damaging for Cathy is the fact that her employees will perceive your move as an act of betrayal—Cathy's so-called friend is raiding her company. They will think, "Cathy is such an ineffective CEO that she cannot even keep her friends from hiring her people." In this way, a logical issue quickly becomes an emotional one.

You don't want to lose Cathy as a friend, so you assure her that Mitchell is the exception and that he came to you and that he will be the first and only one of her employees that joins your company. Generally, this explanation will work and Cathy will understand and appreciate the gesture. She will forgive, but rest assured, she will not forget.

Her memory of Mitchell will be important, because Mitchell will be just the first step in the demise of your relationship. Since Mitchell is a stellar hire, Cathy's other strong employees will likely call Mitchell to understand why he left and where he is going. He will explain his reasoning and his reasons will be compelling. And suddenly they will want to follow Mitchell's path and join your company, too. By the time you become aware of the situation, promises will have been made to prospective employees who approached Mitchell and offers may be out.

In each case, your employees will assure you that they were approached by Cathy's employees and not vice versa. They will point out that the candidates have offers from other companies as well, so they will definitely leave and you might as well benefit from their restlessness. Cathy's managers will almost certainly tell a different story. They will plead with her to get her friend to stop raiding their stable of employees or else they will never be able to meet their commitments. This will embarrass and enrage Cathy. In the end, social pressure will trump all your brilliant countervailing logic.

Here's an easy way to think about the dynamic. If your husband left you, would you want your best friend to date him? He's going to date somebody, so wouldn't you want your friend to have him? It seems logical, but this situation is far from logical and you just lost one friend.

## SO WHAT SHOULD YOU DO?

First, keep in mind that the employees are either extremely good or you probably won't want them in your company anyway. So, you will either be recruiting top-notch employees from your friend's company or you will be adding mediocre people. Do not assume the people you are taking will not be missed.

A good rule of thumb is my Reflexive Principle of Employee Raiding, which states, "If you would be shocked and horrified if Company

X hired several of your employees, then you should not hire any of theirs." The number of such companies should be small and may very well be zero.

In order to avoid these sticky situations, many companies employ written or unwritten policies that name companies where it is not okay to hire without CEO (or senior executive) approval. With such a policy in place, you will be able to give your friend one last chance to save their employee or to object prior to you hiring them.

With that in mind, the best way to deal with these situations is openly and transparently. Once you become aware of the conflict between hiring the superstar employee and double-crossing your valued friend, you should get the issue onto the table by informing the employee that you have an important business relationship with his existing company and you will have to complete a reference check with the CEO prior to extending the offer. Let him know that if he does not want that to happen, then you will stop the process now and keep the process to date confidential. By speaking with your friend before making the hire, you will be able to better judge the relationship impact of hiring her employee. In addition, you may avoid making a bad hire, as often candidates who do well in interviews turn out to be bad employees.

## CLOSING THOUGHTS

In the classic movie *The Good, the Bad and the Ugly,* Clint Eastwood "The Good" and Eli Wallach "The Ugly" are partners in crime. Wallach, a known criminal, has a bounty on his head and the two of them run a scam to collect the reward money. Eastwood turns Wallach in and collects the reward. Then Wallach is sentenced to death by hanging. As Wallach sits on a horse, hands tied behind his back and about to be hanged with a rope around his neck, Eastwood shoots the rope from a distance and frees Wallach and they split the reward money.

This scheme works brilliantly, until one day Eastwood frees Wallach but informs Wallach: "I don't think you'll ever be worth more than three thousand dollars." Wallach retorts, "What do you mean?" Eastwood informs him, "I mean, our partnership is untied. Oh no, not you. You remain tied. I'll keep the money, and you can have the rope." What follows is one of the great revenge pursuits in motion picture history.

So, when you tell your CEO friend that you don't think she'll ever be worth more than this employee, don't expect to stay friends.

# WHY IT'S HARD TO BRING BIG COMPANY EXECS INTO LITTLE COMPANIES

So you've achieved product market fit and you are ready to start building the company. The board encourages you to bring in some "been there, done that" executives who will provide the right financial, sales, and marketing expertise to help you transition from a world-class product to a world-class business. You see a few candidates that you like, but the venture capitalist on the board says, "You are undershooting. This is going to be a huge company. We can attract better talent." So you aim high and bring in a super-accomplished head of sales. This guy has run huge organizations with thousands of employees. He has stellar references and even looks the part. Your VC loves him, because he has an awesome résumé.

## SIX MONTHS LATER . . .

Fast-forward six months and everyone in the company is wondering why the sales (or marketing or finance or product) guy who has produced nothing got such a monster stock option package. Meanwhile, the people doing all the work have much fewer options. Even worse than not getting your money's worth, now the company is in trouble, because you've been missing the numbers as your super-expensive executive sits on his butt. What the frak just happened?

The most important thing to understand is that the job of a big company executive is very different from the job of a small company executive. When I was managing thousands of people at Hewlett-Packard after the sale of Opsware, there was an incredible number of incoming demands on my time. Everyone wanted a piece of me. Little companies wanted to partner with me or sell themselves to me, people in my organization needed approvals, other business units needed my help, customers wanted my attention, and so forth. As a result, I spent most of my time optimizing and tuning the existing business. Most of the work that I did was "incoming." In fact, most skilled big company executives will tell you that if you have more than three new initiatives in a quarter, you are trying to do too much. As a result, big company executives tend to be interrupt-driven.

In contrast, when you are a startup executive, nothing happens unless you make it happen. In the early days of a company, you have to take eight to ten new initiatives a day or the company will stand still. There is no inertia that's putting the company in motion. Without massive input from you, the company will stay at rest.

## SO WHAT HAPPENS?

Once you hire one of these big company executives, there are two dangerous mismatches that you will face:

1. **Rhythm mismatch** Your executive has been conditioned to wait for the emails to come in, wait for the phone to ring, and wait for the meetings to get scheduled. In your company, he will be waiting a long time. If your new executive waits (as per his training), your other employees will become

suspicious. You'll hear things like "What does that guy do all day long?" and "Why did he get so many options?"

2. **Skill set mismatch** Running a large organization requires very different skills than creating and building an organization. When you run a large organization, you tend to become very good at tasks such as complex decision-making, prioritization, organizational design, process improvement, and organizational communication. When you are building an organization, there is no organization to design, there are no processes to improve, and communicating with the organization is simple. On the other hand, you have to be very adept at running a high-quality hiring process, have terrific domain expertise (you are personally responsible for quality control), know how to create process from scratch, and be extremely creative about initiating new directions and tasks.

## HOW CAN YOU STOP THINGS FROM GOING HORRIBLY WRONG?

There are two key steps to avoiding disaster:

1. Screen for devastating mismatches in the interview process.

2. Take integration as seriously as interviewing.

## SCREEN FOR MISMATCHES

How do you tell if the rhythm mismatch or the skill set mismatch will be too much to overcome? Here are some interview questions that I found very helpful:

**What will you do in your first month on the job?**

Beware of answers that overemphasize learning. This may indicate that the candidate thinks there is more to learn about your organization than there actually is. More specifically, he may think that your organization is as complex as his current organization.

Beware of any indication that the candidate needs to be interrupt-driven rather than setting the pace personally. The interrupts will never come.

Look for candidates who come in with more new initiatives than you think are possible. This is a good sign.

**How will your new job differ from your current job?**

Look for self-awareness of the differences here. If they have the experience in what you need, they will be articulate on this point.

Beware of candidates who think that too much of their experience is immediately transferable. It may pay off down the line, but likely not tomorrow.

**Why do you want to join a small company?**

Beware of equity being the primary motivation. One percent of nothing is nothing. That's something that big company executives sometimes have a hard time understanding.

It's much better if they want to be more creative. The most important difference between big and small companies is the amount of time running versus creating. A desire to do more creating is the right reason to want to join your company.

## AGGRESSIVELY INTEGRATE
## THE CANDIDATE ONCE ON BOARD

Perhaps the most critical step is integration. You should plan to spend a huge amount of time integrating any new executive. Here are some things to keep in mind:

- *Force them to create.* Give them monthly, weekly, and even daily objectives to make sure that they produce immediately. The rest of the company will be watching and this will be critical to their assimilation.

- *Make sure that they "get it."* Content-free executives have no value in startups. Every executive must understand the product, the technology, the customers, and the market. Force your newbie to learn these things. Consider scheduling a daily meeting with your new executive. Require them to bring a comprehensive set of questions about everything they heard that day but did not completely understand. Answer those questions in depth; start with first principles. Bring them up to speed fast. If they don't have any questions, consider firing them. If in thirty days you don't feel that they are coming up to speed, definitely fire them.

- *Put them in the mix.* Make sure that they initiate contact and interaction with their peers and other key people in the organization. Give them a list of people they need to know and learn from. Once they've done that, require a report from them on what they learned from each person.

## FINAL THOUGHTS

Nothing will accelerate your company's development like hiring someone who has experience building a very similar company at larger scale. However, doing so can be fraught with peril. Make sure to pay attention to the important leading indicators of success and failure.

# HIRING EXECUTIVES: IF YOU'VE NEVER DONE THE JOB, HOW DO YOU HIRE SOMEBODY GOOD?

The biggest difference between being a great functional manager and being a great general manager—and particularly a great CEO—is that as a general manager, you must hire and manage people who are far more competent at their jobs than you would be at their jobs. In fact, often you will have to hire and manage people to do jobs that you have never done. How many CEOs have been head of HR, engineering, sales, marketing, finance, and legal? Probably none.

So, with no experience, how do you hire someone good?

## STEP 1: KNOW WHAT YOU WANT

Step 1 is definitely the most important step in the process and also the one that gets skipped most often. As the great self-help coach Tony Robbins says, "If you don't know what you want, the chances that you'll get it are extremely low." If you have never done the job, how do you know what to want?

First, you must realize how ignorant you are and resist the temptation to educate yourself simply by interviewing candidates. While the interview process can be highly educational, using that as the sole information source is dangerous. Doing so will make you susceptible to the following traps:

- **Hiring on look and feel** It may seem silly to think that anyone would hire an executive based on the way they look and sound in an interview, but in my experience, look and feel are the top criteria for most executive searches. When you combine a CEO who doesn't know what she wants and a board of directors that hasn't thought much about the hire, what do you think the criteria will be?

- **Looking for someone out of central casting** If I had followed this path, I would never have hired Mark Cranney and you probably would not be reading this now. This wrongheaded approach is the moral equivalent of looking for the Platonic ideal for a head of sales. You imagine what the perfect sales executive might be like, and then you attempt to match real-world candidates to your model. This is a bad idea for several reasons. First, you are not hiring an abstract executive to work at an arbitrary company. You must hire the right person for your company at this particular point in time. The head of sales at Oracle in 2010 would likely have failed in 1989. The VP of engineering at Apple might be exactly the wrong choice for Foursquare. The details and the specifics matter. Second, your imaginary model is almost certainly wrong. What is your basis for creating this model? Finally, it will be incredibly difficult to educate an interview team on such an abstract set of criteria. As a result, everybody will be looking for something different.

- **Valuing lack of weakness rather than strength** The more experience you have, the more you realize that there is something seriously wrong with every employee in your company (including you). Nobody is perfect.

The very best way to know what you want is to act in the role. Not just in title, but in real action. In my career, I've been acting VP of HR, CFO, and VP of sales. Often CEOs resist acting in functional roles, because they worry that they lack the appropriate knowledge. This worry is precisely why you should act—to get the appropriate knowledge. Indeed, acting is really the only way to get all the knowledge that you need to make the hire, because you are looking for the right executive for your company today, not a generic executive.

In addition to acting in the role, it helps greatly to bring in domain experts. If you know a great head of sales, interview them first and learn what they think made them great. Figure out which of those strengths most directly match the needs of your company. If possible, include the domain expert in the interview process. However, be aware that the domain expert only has part of the knowledge necessary to make the hire. Specifically, she has very little knowledge of your company, how it works, and what its needs are. Therefore, you cannot defer the decision to the domain expert.

Finally, be clear in your own mind about your expectations for this person upon joining your company. What will this person do in the first thirty days? What do you expect their motivation to be for joining? Do you want them to build a large organization right away or hire only one or two people over the next year?

## STEP 2. RUN A PROCESS THAT FIGURES OUT THE RIGHT MATCH

In order to find the right executive, you must now take the knowledge that you have gathered and translate it into a process that yields the right candidate. Here is the process that I like to use.

**Write down the strengths you want and the weaknesses that you are willing to tolerate.**

In order to ensure completeness, I find it useful to include criteria from the following subdivisions when hiring executives:

- Will the executive be world-class at running the function?

- Is the executive outstanding operationally?

  □ Will the executive make a major contribution to the strategic direction of the company? This is the "are they smart enough?" criterion.

  □ Will the executive be an effective member of the team? *Effective* is the key word. It's possible for an executive to be well liked and totally ineffective with respect to the other members of the team. It's also possible for an executive to be highly effective and profoundly influential while being totally despised. The latter is far better.

These functions do not carry equal weight for all positions. Make sure that you balance them appropriately. Generally, operational excellence is far more important for a VP of engineering or a VP of sales than for a VP of marketing or a CFO.

**Develop questions that test for the criteria (see the appendix).**

This effort is important even if you never ask the candidate any of the pre-prepared questions. By writing down questions that test for what you want, you will get to a level of specificity that will be extremely difficult to achieve otherwise. (See the appendix for an example of questions that I wrote for running the enterprise sales function and operational excellence.) Assemble an appropriate interview team and conduct the interviews.

**Assemble the interview team.**

In assembling the team, you should keep two questions in mind:

1. Who will best help you figure out whether the candidate meets the criteria? These may be internal or external people. They can be board members, other executives, or just experts.

2. Who do you need to support the decision once the executive is on board? This group is just as important as the first. No matter how great an executive is, they will have trouble succeeding if the people around them sabotage everything they do. The best way to avoid that is to understand any potential issues before the person is hired.

Clearly, some people will be in both groups one and two. The opinions of both groups will be very important: Group one will help you determine the best candidate and group two will help you gauge how easily each candidate will integrate into your company. Generally, it's best to have group two interview finalist candidates only.

Next, assign questions to interviewers based on their talents. Specifically, make sure that the interviewer who asks the questions deeply understands what a good answer will sound like.

As you conduct the interviews, be sure to discuss each interview with the interviewer. Use this time to drive to a common understanding of the criteria, so that you will get the best information possible.

**Backdoor and front-door references.**

For the final candidates, it's critically important that the CEO conduct the reference checks herself. The references need to be checked against the same hiring criteria that you tested for during the interview process. Backdoor reference checks (checks from people who know the candidate, but were not referred by the candidate) can be an extremely useful way to get an unbiased view. However, do not discount the front-door references. While they clearly have committed to giving a positive reference (or they wouldn't be on the list), you are not looking for positive or negative with them. You are looking for fit with your criteria. Often, the front-door references will know the candidate best and will be quite helpful in this respect.

## STEP 3: MAKE A LONELY DECISION

Despite many people being involved in the process, the ultimate decision should be made solo. Only the CEO has comprehensive knowledge of the criteria, the rationale for the criteria, all of the feedback from interviewers and references, and the relative importance of the various stakeholders. Consensus decisions about executives almost always sway the process away from strength and toward lack of weakness. It's a lonely job, but somebody has to do it.

# WHEN EMPLOYEES
# MISINTERPRET MANAGERS

Early on at Loudcloud, many people would do crazy things backed up by "Ben said." Often I didn't say any of it, but I definitely didn't say it in the way they used it. The management principles I share here are connected to many of those experiences.

When I ran Opsware, we had the nonlinear quarter problem also known affectionately as the hockey stick. The hockey stick refers to the shape of the revenue graph over the course of a quarter. Our hockey stick was so bad that one quarter, we booked 90 percent of our new bookings on the last day of the quarter. Sales patterns like this make it difficult to plan the business and are particularly harrowing when you are, as we were, a public company.

Naturally, I was determined to straighten out the hockey stick and bring some sanity to the business. I designed an incentive for salespeople to close deals in the first two months of the quarter by issuing bonuses for deals in those months. As a result, the next quarter became slightly more linear, and slightly smaller than anticipated—deals just moved from the third month to the first two of the following quarter.

When I ran a large engineering group at Netscape, I measured one of our engineering products on schedule, quality, and features. The team shipped a product with all the required features, on time and with very few bugs. Unfortunately, the product was mediocre, because none of the features were that great.

When I was at HP, we ran all the businesses by the numbers with extremely strict revenue and margin targets. Some divisions made their numbers, but did so by underfunding R&D. They dramatically weakened their long-term competitive position and set themselves up for future disaster.

In all three cases, managers got what we asked for, but not what we wanted. How did this happen? Let's take a look.

## FLATTENING OUT THE HOCKEY STICK: THE WRONG GOAL

In retrospect, I should never have asked the team to flatten the quarters. If that is what I wanted, I had to be willing to—at least temporarily—accept smaller quarters. We had a fixed number of salespeople who were maximizing the size of each quarter. In order to deliver linear quarters, they had to modify their behavior and adjust their priorities. Unfortunately, I liked the old priority of maximizing revenue better.

Given the situation, I was actually pretty lucky. Sun Tzu, in his classic work *The Art of War*, warns that giving the team a task that it cannot possibly perform is called crippling the army. In my case, I did not cripple the team, but I screwed up my priorities. The right thing to do would have been to make the hard decision up front, about what was more important, maximizing each quarter or increasing predictability. The instruction only made sense if the answer was the second one.

## FOCUSING TOO MUCH ON THE NUMBERS

In the second example, I managed the team to a set of numbers that did not fully capture what I wanted. I wanted a great product that customers would love with high quality and on time—in that order.

Unfortunately, the metrics that I set did not capture those priorities. At a basic level, metrics are incentives. By measuring quality, features, and schedule and discussing them at every staff meeting, my people focused intensely on those metrics to the exclusion of other goals. The metrics did not describe the real goals and I distracted the team as a result.

Interestingly, I see this same problem play out in many consumer Internet startups. I often see teams that maniacally focus on their metrics around customer acquisition and retention. This usually works well for customer acquisition, but not so well for retention. Why?

For many products, metrics often describe the customer acquisition goal in enough detail to provide sufficient management guidance. In contrast, the metrics for customer retention do not provide enough color to be a complete management tool. As a result, many young companies overemphasize retention metrics and do not spend enough time going deep enough on the actual user experience. This generally results in a frantic numbers chase that does not end in a great product. It's important to supplement a great product vision with a strong discipline around the metrics, but if you substitute metrics for product vision, you will not get what you want.

## MANAGING STRICTLY BY NUMBERS IS LIKE PAINTING BY NUMBERS

Some things that you want to encourage will be quantifiable, and some will not. If you report on the quantitative goals and ignore the qualitative ones, you won't get the qualitative goals, which may be the most important ones. Management purely by numbers is sort of like painting by numbers—it's strictly for amateurs.

At HP, the company wanted high earnings now and in the future. By focusing entirely on the numbers, HP got them now by sacrificing the future.

Note that there were many numbers as well as more qualitative goals that would have helped:

- Was our competitive win rate increasing or declining?

- Was customer satisfaction rising or falling?

- What did our own engineers think of the products?

By managing the organization as though it were a black box, some divisions at HP optimized the present at the expense of their down-stream competitiveness. The company rewarded managers for achieving short-term objectives in a manner that was bad for the company. It would have been better to take into account the white box. The white box goes beyond the numbers and gets into how the organization produced the numbers. It penalizes managers who sacrifice the future for the short term and rewards those who invest in the future even if that investment cannot be easily measured.

## CLOSING THOUGHT

It is easy to see that there are many ways for leaders to be misinterpreted. To get things right, you must recognize that anything you measure automatically creates a set of employee behaviors. Once you determine the result you want, you need to test the description of the result against the employee behaviors that the description will likely create. Otherwise, the side-effect behaviors may be worse than the situation you were trying to fix.

# MANAGEMENT DEBT

Thanks to Ward Cunningham, the computer programmer who designed the first wiki, the metaphor "technical debt" is now a well-understood concept. While you may be able to borrow time by writing quick and dirty code, you will eventually have to pay it back—with interest. Often this trade-off makes sense, but you will run into serious trouble if you fail to keep the trade-off in the front of your mind. There also exists a less understood parallel concept, which I will call *management debt*.

Like technical debt, management debt is incurred when you make an expedient, short-term management decision with an expensive, long-term consequence. Like technical debt, the trade-off sometimes makes sense, but often does not. More important, if you incur the management debt without accounting for it, then you will eventually go management bankrupt.

Like technical debt, management debt comes in too many different forms to elaborate entirely, but a few salient examples will help explain the concept. Here are three of the more popular types among startups:

1. Putting two in the box

2. Overcompensating a key employee, because she gets another job offer

3. No performance management or employee feedback process

## PUTTING TWO IN THE BOX

What do you do when you have two outstanding employees who logically both fit in the same place on the organizational chart? Perhaps you have a world-class architect who is running engineering, but she does not have the experience to scale the organization to the next level. You also have an outstanding operational person who is not great technically. You want to keep both in the company, but you only have one position. So you get the bright idea to put "two in the box" and take on a little management debt. The short-term benefits are clear: you keep both employees, you don't have to develop either because they will theoretically help each other develop, and you instantly close the skill set gap. Unfortunately, you will pay for those benefits with interest and at a very high rate.

For starters, by doing this you will make every engineer's job more difficult. If an engineer needs a decision made, which boss should she go to? If that boss decides, will the other boss be able to override it? If it's a complex decision that requires a meeting, does she have to schedule both heads of engineering for the meeting? Who sets the direction for the organization? Will the direction actually get set if doing so requires a series of meetings?

In addition, you have removed all accountability. If schedules slip, who is accountable? If engineering throughput becomes uncompetitive, who is responsible? If the operational head is responsible for the schedule slip and the technical head is responsible for throughput, what happens if the operational head thrashes the engineers to make the schedule and kills throughput? How would you know that she did that? The really expensive part about both of these things is that they tend to get worse over time. In the very short term you might mitigate their effects with extra meetings or by attempting to carve up the job in a clear way. However, as things get busy, those once-clear lines will fade and the organization will degenerate. Eventually, you'll either make a lump-sum payment by making the hard decision and putting one in the box or your engineering organization will suck forever.

## OVERCOMPENSATING A KEY EMPLOYEE BECAUSE SHE GETS ANOTHER JOB OFFER

An excellent engineer decides to leave the company because she gets a better offer. For various reasons, you were undercompensating her, but the offer from the other company pays more than any engineer in your company and the engineer in question is not your best engineer. Still, she is working on a critical project and you cannot afford to lose her. So you match the offer. You save the project, but you pile on the debt.

Here's how the payment will come due. You probably think that your counteroffer was confidential because you'd sworn her to secrecy. Let me explain why it was not. She has friends in the company. When she got the offer from the other company, she consulted with her friends. One of her best friends advised her to take the offer. When she decided to stay, she had to explain to him why she disregarded his advice or else lose personal credibility. So she told him and swore him to secrecy. He agreed to honor the secret but was incensed that she had to threaten to quit in order to get a proper raise. Furthermore, he was furious that you overcompensated her. So he told the story to a few of his friends, but kept her name confidential to preserve the secret. And now everyone in engineering knows that the best way to get a raise is to generate an offer from another company and then threaten to quit. It's going to take a while to pay off that debt.

## NO PERFORMANCE MANAGEMENT OR
## EMPLOYEE FEEDBACK PROCESS

Your company now employs twenty-five people and you know that you should formalize the performance management process, but you don't want to pay the price. You worry that doing so will make it feel like a "big company." Moreover, you do not want your employees to be offended by the feedback, because you can't afford to lose anyone right now. And people are happy, so why rock the boat? Why not take on a little management debt?

The first noticeable payments will be due when somebody performs below expectations:

CEO: "He was good when we hired him; what happened?"

Manager: "He's not doing the things that we need him to do."

CEO: "Did we clearly tell him that?"

Manager: "Maybe not clearly . . ."

However, the larger payment will be a silent tax. Companies execute well when everybody is on the same page and everybody is constantly improving. In a vacuum of feedback, there is almost no chance that your company will perform optimally across either dimension. Directions with no corrections will seem fuzzy and obtuse. People rarely improve weakness they are unaware of. The ultimate price you will pay for not giving feedback: systematically crappy company performance.

## IN THE END

Every really good, really experienced CEO I know shares one important characteristic: They tend to opt for the hard answer to organizational issues. If faced with giving everyone the same bonus to make things easy or with sharply rewarding performance and ruffling many feathers, they'll ruffle the feathers. If given the choice of cutting a popular project today, because it's not in the long-term plans or you're keeping it around for morale purposes and to appear consistent, they'll cut it today. Why? Because they've paid the price of management debt, and they would rather not do that again.

# MANAGEMENT QUALITY ASSURANCE

Everyone in the technology industry seems to agree that people are paramount, yet nobody seems to be on the same page with what the people organization—human resources—should look like.

The problem is that when it comes to HR, most CEOs don't really know what they want. In theory, they want a well-managed company with a great culture. Instinctively they know that an HR organization probably can't deliver that. As a result, CEOs usually punt on the issue and implement something that's suboptimal, if not worthless.

Ironically one of the first things you learn when you run an engineering organization is that a good quality assurance organization cannot build a high-quality product, but it can tell you when the development team builds a low quality product. Similarly, a high quality human resources organization cannot make you a well-managed company with a great culture, but it can tell you when you and your managers are not getting the job done.

## THE EMPLOYEE LIFE CYCLE

The best way to approach management quality assurance is through the lens of the employee life cycle. From hire to retire, how good is your company? Is your management team world-class in all phases? How do you know?

A great HR organization will support, measure, and help improve your management team. Some of the questions they will help you answer:

### Recruiting and Hiring

- Do you sharply understand the skills and talents required to succeed in every open position?

- Are your interviewers well prepared?

- Do your managers and employees do an effective job of selling your company to prospective employees?

- Do interviewers arrive on time?

- Do managers and recruiters follow up with candidates in a timely fashion?

- Do you compete effectively for talent against the best companies?

### Compensation

- Do your benefits make sense for your company demographics?

- How do your salary and stock option packages compare with the companies that you compete with for talent?

- How well do your performance rankings correspond to your compensation practices?

### Training and Integration

- When you hire an employee, how long does it take them to become productive from the perspective of the employee, her peers, and her manager?

- Shortly after joining, how well does an employee understand what's expected of her?

### Performance Management

- Do your managers give consistent, clear feedback to their employees?

- What is the quality of your company's written performance reviews?

- Did all of your employees receive their reviews on time?

- Do you effectively manage out poor performers?

### Motivation

- Are your employees excited to come to work?

- Do your employees believe in the mission of the company?

- Do they enjoy coming to work every day?

- Do you have any employees who are actively disengaged?

- Do your employees clearly understand what's expected of them?

- Do employees stay a long time or do they quit faster than normal?

- Why do employees quit?

## REQUIREMENTS TO BE GREAT AT RUNNING HR

What kind of person should you look for to comprehensively and continuously understand the quality of your management team? Here are some key requirements:

- **World-class process design skills** Much like the head of quality assurance, the head of HR must be a masterful process designer. One key to accurately measuring critical management processes is excellent process design and control.

- **A true diplomat** Nobody likes a tattletale and there is no way for an HR organization to be effective if the management team doesn't implicitly trust it. Managers must believe that HR is there to help them improve rather than police them. Great HR leaders genuinely want to help the managers and couldn't care less about getting credit for identifying problems. They will work directly with the managers to get quality up and only escalate to the CEO when necessary. If an HR leader hoards knowledge, makes power plays, or plays politics, he will be useless.

- **Industry knowledge** Compensation, benefits, best recruiting practices, etc. are all fast-moving targets. The head of HR must be deeply networked in the industry and stay abreast of all the latest developments.

- **Intellectual heft to be the CEO's trusted adviser** None of the other skills matter if the CEO does not fully back the head of HR in holding the managers to a high quality standard. In order for this to happen, the CEO must trust the HR leader's thinking and judgment.

- **Understanding things unspoken** When management quality starts to break down in a company, nobody says anything about it, but super-perceptive people can tell that the company is slipping. You need one of those.

# CHAPTER 6

# CONCERNING THE GOING CONCERN

"This ain't for no fuck niggas
If you a real nigga then fuck with me."
—TRINIDAD JAMES, "ALL GOLD EVERYTHING"

One day in a staff meeting in the Loudcloud/Opsware days, someone brought up an issue that had been bothering him for some time. "This place is entirely too profane. It's making many of the employees uncomfortable." Others chimed in: "It makes the environment unprofessional. We need to put a stop to it." Although the complaints were abstract, they were clearly directed at me since I was the biggest abuser of profanity in the company and perhaps in the industry. In those days, I directed the team with such urgency that it was rare for me to say more than a few sentences without an expletive injected somewhere.

Part of it was intentional. I only had so much time with each employee and it was critically important that I be crystal clear in those moments. Nothing makes things clear like a few choice curse words. "That is not the priority" is radically weaker than "That is not the fucking priority." When the CEO drops the F-bomb, it gets repeated. And that's good if you want your message to spread throughout the company. (On the other hand, it's extremely bad if you don't want your employees talking like a bunch of gangsta rappers.) But part of it was also unintentional. At this point, I could barely control myself. This was not an easy company to run, and I'd developed CEO Tourette's syndrome—the profanity was involuntary.

Since the complaints seemed broad and deep, I had to take them seriously. I thought hard about it that night and considered the following.

- In the technology business, some employees would be comfortable with profanity while others would not.

- If we outlawed profanity, then some employees who used it would not come to work for us or quit once they got there because we would seem old-fashioned and prudish.

- If we kept profanity, some people might leave.

- My judgment was biased, because I was the main offender.

After much consideration, I realized that the best technology companies of the day, Intel and Microsoft, were known to be highly profane places, so we'd be off culture with them and the rest of the modern industry if we stopped profanity. Obviously, that didn't mean that we had to encourage it, but prohibiting it seemed both unrealistic and counterproductive. Attracting the very best engineers meant recruiting from highly profane environments. The choice was between optimizing for top talent or clean culture. Easy decision.

I decided to keep the cursing, but I also needed to make a statement. People had complained and had run this issue all the way up the organization, and they deserved an explanation. Explaining things would be tricky, because profanity did not work in all contexts. We certainly could not tolerate profanity used to intimidate or sexually harass employees, so I needed to make the distinction clear. Approving profanity only in certain contexts was a tricky message to craft.

That night I watched a disturbing movie from the late 1970s called

*Short Eyes*, which told the graphic story of a child molester who went to prison and confronted the one clear prison ethic: Child molesters must die. One of the characters in the movie was a young man referred to by the other inmates as "Cupcakes."

Hard to believe, but watching that movie, I found my solution.

The next day, I gave the following speech at the all-company meeting:

"It has come to my attention that many people are uncomfortable with the amount of profanity that we use. Being the number-one abuser, these complaints have caused me to reflect on my own behavior as well as the company as a whole. As I see it, we have two choices: (a) we can ban profanity or (b) we can accept profanity. Anything in between is very unlikely to work. 'Minimal profanity' cannot be enforced. I've said before that we cannot win unless we attract the very best people in the world. In the technology industry, almost everybody comes from a culture that allows profanity. Therefore, banning profanity will likely limit our talent pool more than accepting profanity. As a result, we will allow profanity. However, this does not mean that you can use profanity to intimidate, sexually harass people, or do other bad things. In this way, profanity is no different from other language. For example, consider the word 'cupcakes.' It's fine for me to say to Shannon, 'Those cupcakes you baked look delicious.' But it is not okay for me to say to Anthony, 'Hey, Cupcakes, you look mighty fine in them jeans.'"

And that was all I said about that.

After that day, I never heard another complaint about profanity and I don't think we lost anybody because of the policy. Sometimes an organization doesn't need a solution; it just needs clarity. Once I made it clear that cursing was okay—so long as it wasn't used to intimidate or harass—nobody had a problem with it anymore. At least as far as I knew. Bottom line, the results of the policy were good: a comfortable work environment, low attrition, and no complaining. Sometimes the right policy is the one that the CEO can follow.

As a company grows, it will change. No matter how well you set your culture, keep your spirit, or slow-roll your growth, your company won't be the same when it's one thousand people as it was when it was ten people. But that doesn't mean that it can't be a good company when it reaches 1,000, 10,000, or even 100,000 employees. It will just be different. Making it good at scale means admitting that it must be different and embracing the changes that you'll need to make to keep things from falling apart. This chapter explains some of the changes that you will need to make.

# HOW TO MINIMIZE POLITICS
# IN YOUR COMPANY

In all my years in business, I have yet to hear someone say, "I love corporate politics." On the other hand, I meet plenty of people who complain bitterly about corporate politics—sometimes even in the companies they run. So, if nobody loves politics, why all the politics?

Political behavior almost always starts with the CEO. Now you may be thinking, "I hate politics, I'm not political, but my organization is very political. I clearly didn't cause this." Sadly, you needn't be political to create extreme political behavior in your organization. In fact, it's often the least political CEOs who run the most ferociously political organizations. Apolitical CEOs frequently—and accidentally—encourage intense political behavior.

What do I mean by politics? I mean people advancing their careers or agendas by means other than merit and contribution. There may be other types of politics, but politics of this form seem to be the ones that really bother people.

## HOW IT HAPPENS

A CEO creates politics by encouraging and sometimes incentivizing political behavior—often unintentionally. As a very simple example, let's consider executive compensation. When you are CEO, senior employees will come to you from time to time and ask for an increase in compensation. They may suggest that you are paying them far less than their current market value. They may even have a competitive offer in hand. Faced with this confrontation, if the request is reasonable, you might investigate the situation. You might even give the employee a raise. This may sound innocent, but you have just created a strong incentive for political behavior.

Specifically, you will be rewarding behavior that has nothing to do with advancing your business. The employee will earn a raise by asking for one rather than as a result of your rewarding them for outstanding performance. Why is this bad? Let me count the ways:

1. The other ambitious members of your staff will immediately get the point and agitate for raises as well. Word always gets out. Note that neither this campaign nor the prior one need be correlated with actual performance. You will now spend time dealing with the political issues rather than actual performance issues. Importantly, if you have a competent board, you will not be able to give them all out-of-cycle raises, so your company executive raises will occur on a first-come, first-served basis.

2. The less aggressive (but perhaps more competent) members of your team will be denied off-cycle raises simply by being apolitical.

3. The object lesson for your staff and the company will be that the squeaky wheel gets the grease, and that the most politically astute employees get the raises. Get ready for a whole lot of squeaky wheels.

Now let's move on to a more complicated example. Your CFO comes to you and says that he wants to continue developing as a manager. He says that he would like to eventually become a COO and would like to know what skills he must demonstrate in order to earn that position in your company. Being a positive leader, you would like to encourage him to pursue his dream. You tell him that you think that he'd be a fine COO someday and that he should work to develop a few more skills. In addition, you tell him that he'll need to be a strong enough leader, such that other executives in the company will want to work for him. A week later, one of your other executives comes to you in a panic. She says that the CFO just asked her if she'd work for him. She says that he said you are grooming him to be the COO and that's his final step. Did that just happen? Welcome to the big time.

## HOW TO MINIMIZE POLITICS

Minimizing politics often feels totally unnatural. It's counter to excellent management practices such as being open-minded and encouraging employee development.

The difference between managing executives and managing more junior employees can be thought of as the difference between being in a fight with someone with no training and being in a ring with a professional boxer. If you are in a fight with a regular person, then you can do natural things and they won't get you into much trouble. For example, if you want to take a step backward, you can pick your front foot up first. If you do this against a professional boxer, you will get your block knocked off. Professional boxers train for years to take advantage of small errors in technique. Lifting your front foot first to take a step backward will take you slightly off balance for a split second and that's all your opponent will need.

Similarly, if you manage a junior employee and they ask you about their career development, you can say what comes naturally and generally get away with it. As we saw above, things change when you deal with highly ambitious, seasoned professionals. In order to keep from getting knocked out by corporate politics, you need to refine your technique.

## THE TECHNIQUE

As I developed as a CEO, I found two key techniques to be useful in minimizing politics.

1. Hire people with the right kind of ambition. The cases that I described above might involve people who are ambitious but not necessarily inherently political. All cases are not like this. The surest way to turn your company into the political equivalent of the U.S. Senate is to hire people with the wrong kind of ambition. As defined by Andy Grove, the right kind of ambition is ambition for the company's success with the executive's own success only coming as a by-product of the company's victory. The wrong kind of ambition is ambition for the executive's personal success regardless of the company's outcome.

2. Build strict processes for potentially political issues and do not deviate. Certain activities attract political behavior. These activities include:

    □ Performance evaluation and compensation

    □ Organizational design and territory

    □ Promotions

Let's examine each case and how you might build and execute a process that insulates the company from bad behavior and politically motivated outcomes.

**Performance evaluation and compensation** Often companies defer putting performance management and compensation processes in place. This doesn't mean that they don't evaluate employees or give pay raises; it just means they do so in an ad hoc manner that's highly vulnerable to political machinations. By conducting well-structured, regular performance and compensation reviews, you will ensure that pay and stock increases are as fair as possible. This is especially important for executive compensation, since doing so will also serve to minimize politics. In the example above, the CEO should have had an airtight performance and compensation policy and simply told the executive that his compensation would be evaluated with everyone else's. Ideally, the executive compensation process should involve the board of directors. This will help ensure good governance and make exceptions even more difficult.

**Organizational design and territory** If you manage ambitious people, from time to time they will want to expand their scope of responsibility. In the example above, the CFO wanted to become the COO. In other situations, the head of marketing might want to run sales and marketing or the head of engineering may want to run engineering and product management. When someone raises an issue like this with you, you must be very careful about what you say, because everything that you say can be turned into political cannon fodder. Generally, it's best to say nothing at all. At most, you might ask "why?" but if you do so be sure not to react to the reasons. If you indicate what you are thinking, that information will leak, rumors will spread, and you plant the seeds for all kinds of unproductive discussions. You should evaluate your organizational design on a regular basis and gather the information that you need to decide without tipping people off to what you plan to do. Once you decide, you should immediately execute the reorg: Don't leave time for leaks and lobbying.

**Promotions** Every time your company gives someone a promotion, everyone else at that person's organizational level evaluates the promotion and judges whether merit or political favors yielded it. If the latter, then the other employees generally react in one of three ways:

1. They sulk and feel undervalued.

2. They outwardly disagree, campaign against the person, and undermine them in their new position.

3. They attempt to copy the political behavior that generated the unwarranted promotion.

Clearly, you don't want any of these behaviors in your company. Therefore, you must have a formal, visible, defensible promotion process that governs every employee promotion. Often this process must be different for people on your own staff. (The general process may involve various managers who are familiar with the employee's work; the executive process should include the board of directors.) The purpose of the process is twofold. First, it will give the organization confidence that the company at least attempted to base the promotion on merit. Second, the process will produce the information necessary for your team to explain the promotion decisions you made.

**Be careful with "he said, she said"** Once your organization grows to a significant size, members of your team will from time to time complain about each other. Sometimes this criticism will be extremely aggressive. Be careful about how you listen and the message that it sends. Simply by hearing them out without defending the employee in question, you will send the message that you agree. If people in the company think that you agree that one of your executives is less than stellar, that information will spread quickly and without qualification. As a result, people will stop listening to the executive in question and the executive will soon become ineffective.

There are two distinct types of complaints that you will receive:

1. Complaints about an executive's behavior

2. Complaints about an executive's competency or performance

Generally, the best way to handle the first type of complaint is to get the complaining executive and the targeted executive in the room together and have them explain themselves. Usually, simply having this meeting will resolve the conflict and correct the behavior and improve the relationship (if it was actually broken). Do not attempt to address behavioral issues without both executives in the room. Doing so will invite manipulation and politics.

Complaints of the second type are both more rare and more complex. If one of your executives summons the courage to complain about the competency of one of their peers, then there is a good chance that either the complainer or the targeted executive has a major problem. If you receive this type of complaint, you will generally have one of two reactions: they will be telling you something that you already know, or they'll be telling you shocking news.

If they are telling you something that you already know, then the big news is that you have let the situation go too far. Whatever your reasons for attempting to rehabilitate the wayward executive, you have taken too long and now your organization has turned on them. You must resolve the situation quickly. Almost always, this means firing the executive. While I've seen executives improve their performance and skill sets, I've never seen one lose the support of the organization and then regain it.

On the other hand, if the complaint is new news, then you must immediately stop the conversation and make clear to the complaining executive that you in no way agree with their assessment. You do not want to cripple the other executive before you reevaluate his performance. You do not want the complaint to become a self-fulfilling prophecy. Once you've shut down the conversation, you must quickly reassess the employee in question. If you find he is doing an excellent job, you must figure out the complaining executive's motivations and resolve them. Do not let an accusation of this magnitude fester. If you find that the employee is doing a poor job, there will be time to go back and get the complaining employee's input, but you should be on a track to remove the poor performer at that point.

As CEO, you must consider the systemic incentives that result from your words and actions. While it may feel good in the moment to be open, responsive, and action oriented, be careful not to encourage all the wrong things.

# THE RIGHT KIND OF AMBITION

When hiring a management team, most startups focus almost exclusively on IQ, but a bunch of high-IQ people with the wrong kind of ambition won't work. I have already stressed that you should strive to hire people with the right kind of ambition. As I've talked about these ideas in the last few years, I have received a mixed response. Some think it's good advice, while others question it.

At a macro level, a company will be most successful if the senior managers optimize for the company's success (think of this as a global optimization) as opposed to their own personal success (local optimization). No matter how well the CEO designs the personal incentive programs, they will never be perfect. In addition, career incentives like promotions and territory ownership fall outside the scope of bonus plans and other a priori management tools. In an equity-based compensation structure, optimizing for the company's success should yield better results for individuals as well. As my Opsware head of sales Mark Cranney used to say, "Two percent of zero is zero."

It is particularly important that managers have the right kind of ambition, because anything else will be exceptionally demotivating for their employees. As an employee, why would I want to work long hours to advance the career of my manager? If the manager cares more about his career than the company, then that's what I'd be doing. Nothing motivates a great employee more than a mission that's so important that it supersedes everyone's personal ambition. As a result, managers with the right kind of ambition tend to be radically more valuable than those with the wrong kind. For a complete explanation of the dangers of managers with the wrong kind of ambition, I strongly recommend Dr. Seuss's management masterpiece *Yertle the Turtle.*

## SCREENING FOR THE RIGHT
## KIND OF AMBITION

As with any complex character trait, there is no way to perfectly screen for the right kind of ambition in an interview, but hopefully some of these thoughts will prove useful.

At a macro level, everybody views the world through her own personal prism. When interviewing candidates, it's helpful to watch for small distinctions that indicate whether they view the world through the "me" prism or the "team" prism.

People who view the world through the "me" prism might describe a prior company's failure in an interview as follows: "My last job was my e-commerce play. I felt that it was important to round out my résumé." Note the use of *my* to personalize the company in a way that it's unlikely that anyone else at the company would agree with. In fact, the other employees in the company might even be offended by this usage. People with the right kind of ambition would not likely use the word *play* to describe their effort to work as a team to build something substantial. Finally, people who use the "me" prism find it natural and obvious to speak in terms of "building out my résumé" while people who use the "team" prism find such phrases to be somewhat uncomfortable and awkward, because they clearly indicate an individual goal that is separate from the team goal.

On the other hand, people who view the world purely through the team prism will very seldom use the words *I* or *me* even when answering questions about their accomplishments. Even in an inter-view, they will deflect credit to others on their previous team. They will tend to be far more interested in how your company will win than in how they will be compensated or what their career path will be. When asked about a previously failed company, they will generally feel such great responsibility that they will describe in detail their own misjudgments and bad decisions.

When we hired the head of worldwide sales for Opsware, using this screen proved to be quite valuable. Since this was a sales position, I should mention (in reference to the commenter above) that ambition for the company above one's own goals is particularly important for the head of sales. The reasons are many:

- The local incentives in sales are particularly strong and dif-ficult to balance without the right kind of leadership.

- The sales organization is the face of the company to the out-side world. If that group optimizes for itself, your company will have a major problem.

- In high-tech companies, fraud generally starts in sales due to managers attempting to perfect the ultimate local optimization.

Throughout our interview process, we met with a lot of candi-dates who took sole credit for landing extremely large deals, achiev-ing impressive goals, and generating company success. Invariably, the candidates who claimed the most credit for deals would have the most difficult time describing the details of how the deal was actually won and orchestrated. During reference checks, others involved in the deals would tell a very different story.

When I spoke to Mark Cranney, on the other hand, it was difficult to get him to discuss his personal accomplishments. In fact, some of the other interviewers felt that Mark was standoffish and even ob-noxious in the way he bristled at certain questions. One interviewer complained, "Ben, I know that he increased the size of the Nike deal from one million to five million, because our contact at Nike told me that, but Mark wouldn't go into any detail on it." When I interviewed Mark, he really only wanted to discuss how his old company won. He went into great detail about how his team diagnosed weaknesses versus the competition and how he worked with another executive to advance the product. He then talked about how he worked with the CEO to revise the way the sales force was trained and organized.

When the conversation turned to Opsware, Mark had already interviewed sales reps at our number-one competitor's company and knew what deals they were in. He relentlessly questioned me on how we were going to win the deals that they were in and how we planned to get into the deals that we weren't in. He wanted to know the strengths and weaknesses of everyone else on the team. He wanted to know the game plan for winning. The topics of his potential compensation and career advancement didn't come up until the very end of the process. And then he only wanted assurances that compensation was performance- and not politically based. It was clear that Mark was all about the team and its success.

During Mark's tenure, sales increased more than tenfold, and our market capitalization increased twentyfold. More to the point, voluntary attrition in the sales organization was extremely low, customers were managed fairly and honestly, and our legal and finance teams often commented that first and foremost, Mark protected the company.

## FINAL THOUGHT

While it may work to have individual employees who optimize for their own careers, counting on senior managers to do all the right things for all the wrong reasons is a dangerous idea.

# TITLES AND PROMOTIONS

Often when I meet with startups, the employees have no job titles. This makes sense, because everybody is just working to build the company. Roles needn't be clearly defined and, in fact, can't be, because everyone does a little bit of everything. In an environment like this there are no politics and nobody is jockeying for position or authority. It's rather nice. So why do all organizations eventually create job titles and what is the proper way to manage them? (Thanks to Mark Zuckerberg for contributing to my thinking on this subject.)

## WHY DO TITLES MATTER?

Two important factors drive all companies to eventually create job titles:

1. *Employees want them.* While you may plan to work at your company forever, at least some of your employees need to plan for life after your company. When your head of sales interviews for her next job, she won't want to say that despite the fact that she ran a global sales force with hundreds of employees, her title was "Dude."

2. *Eventually, people need to know who is who.* As companies grow, everybody won't know everybody else. Importantly, employees won't know what each person does and whom they should work with to get their jobs done. Job titles provide an excellent shorthand for describing roles in the company. In addition, customers and business partners can also make use of this shorthand to figure out how to best work with your company.

Beyond these core reasons, employees will use titles to calibrate their value and compensation against their colleagues. If an employee with a title of Junior Engineer believes that she is a far better programmer than her counterpart with the title Senior Architect, this will indicate to her that she may be underpaid and undervalued. Because titles will be used to calculate relative value, they must be managed carefully.

## THE DANGERS: THE PETER PRINCIPLE AND THE LAW OF CRAPPY PEOPLE

The basics seem obvious, so why does almost every company eventually make serious mistakes regarding titles? If you have ever worked in a company, you have probably thought to yourself about some overly promoted executive: "How did he get to be a vice president? I wouldn't let him manage a lemonade stand."

One challenge is the Peter Principle. Coined by Dr. Laurence J. Peter and Raymond Hull in their 1969 book of that name, the Peter Principle holds that in a hierarchy, members are promoted so long as they work competently. Sooner or later they are promoted to a position at which they are no longer competent (their "level of incompetence"), and there they remain being unable to earn further promotions. As Andy Grove points out in his management classic *High Output Management*, the Peter Principle is unavoidable, because there is no way to know a priori at what level in the hierarchy a manager will be incompetent.

Another challenge is a phenomenon that I call the *Law of Crappy People*. The Law of Crappy People states: *For any title level in a large organization, the talent on that level will eventually converge to the crappiest person with the title.*

The rationale behind the law is that the other employees in the company with lower titles will naturally benchmark themselves against the crappiest person at the next level. For example, if Jasper is the worst vice president in the company, then all of the directors will benchmark themselves against Jasper and demand promotions as soon as they reach his low level of competency.

As with the Peter Principle, the best that you can do is to mitigate the Law of Crappy People and that mitigation will be critically important to the quality of your company.


## PROMOTION PROCESS

The best way to mitigate both the Peter Principle and the Law of Crappy People is with a properly constructed and highly disciplined promotion process. Ideally, the promotion process should yield a result similar to the very best karate dojos. In top dojos, in order to achieve the next level (for example, being promoted from a brown belt to a black belt), you must defeat an opponent in combat at that level. This guarantees that a new black belt is never a worse fighter than the worst current black belt.

Frustratingly, there is no exact analogue to a fistfight in business, so how can we preserve quality without actual combat?

To begin, start with an extremely crisp definition not only of the responsibilities at each level but also of the skill required to perform the duties. When describing the skills, avoid the generic characterizations such as "must be competent at managing a P&L" or "must have excellent management skills." In fact, the best leveling tools get extremely specific and even name names: "should be a superstar recruiter—as good as Jenny Rogers."

Next, define a formal process for all promotions. One key requirement of the process should be that promotions will be leveled across groups. If you let a manager or a single chain of command determine promotions unilaterally, then it's possible that, for example, HR will have five vice presidents and Engineering only one. One way to level across groups is to hold a regular promotions council that reviews every significant promotion in the company. When a manager wishes to promote an employee, she will submit that employee for review with an explanation of why she believes her employee satisfies the skill criteria required for the level. The committee should then compare the employee with both the level's skill description and the skills of the other employees at that level to determine whether to approve the promotion. In addition to ensuring fairness and level quality, this process will serve to educate your entire management team on the skills and accomplishments of the employees being submitted for promotion.


## ANDREESSEN VS. ZUCKERBERG: HOW BIG SHOULD THE TITLES BE?

Should your company make Vice President the top title or should you have Chief Marketing Officers, Chief Revenue Officers, Chief People Officers, and Chief Snack Officers? There are two schools of thought regarding this, one represented by Marc Andreessen and the other by Mark Zuckerberg.

Andreessen argues that people ask for many things from a company: salary, bonus, stock options, span of control, and titles. Of those, title is by far the cheapest, so it makes sense to give the highest titles possible. The hierarchy should have Presidents, Chiefs, and Senior Executive Vice Presidents. If it makes people feel better, let them feel better. Titles cost nothing. Better yet, when competing for new employees with other companies, using Andreessen's method you can always outbid the competition in at least one dimension.

At Facebook, by contrast, Mark Zuckerberg purposely deploys titles that are significantly lower than the industry standard. Senior Vice Presidents at other companies must take title haircuts down to Directors or Managers at Facebook. Why does he do this? First, he guarantees that every new employee gets releveled as they enter his company. In this way, he avoids accidentally giving new employees higher titles and positions than better-performing existing employees. This boosts morale and increases fairness. Second, it forces all the managers of Facebook to understand and internalize Facebook's leveling system, which serves the company extremely well in their own promotion and compensation processes.

He also wants titles to be meaningful and reflect who has influence in the organization. As a company grows quickly, it's important to provide organizational clarity wherever possible and that gets more difficult if there are fifty VPs and ten Chiefs.

Next, he finds that businesspeople often carry inflated titles versus their engineering counterparts. While he recognizes that big titles help them out externally with getting meetings, he still wants to have an organization where the product people and engineers form the cultural core, so he strives to keep this in check as well.

Does Facebook ever miss out on a new hire due to its low titles? Yes, definitely. But one might argue that they miss out on precisely the employees they don't want. In fact, both the hiring and onboarding processes at Facebook have been carefully designed to encourage the right kind of employees to select themselves in and the wrong ones to select themselves out.

So which method is better, Andreessen's or Zuckerberg's? The answer is that it depends. Facebook has so many advantages in recruiting employees that being disciplined about absolute title levels does not significantly impair its ability to attract the very best talent.

Your company might not have these advantages, so lofty titles may be a good tactic. In either scenario, you should still run a highly disciplined internal leveling and promotion process.

## FINAL THOUGHT

You might think that so much time spent on promotions and titles places too much importance and focus on silly formalisms. The opposite is true. Without a well thought out, disciplined process for titles and promotions, your employees will become obsessed with the resulting inequities. If you structure things properly, nobody other than you will spend much time thinking about titles other than Employee of the Month.

# WHEN SMART PEOPLE ARE BAD EMPLOYEES

In business, intelligence is always a critical element in any employee, because what we do is difficult and complex and the competitors are filled with extremely smart people. However, intelligence is not the only important quality. Being effective in a company also means working hard, being reliable, and being an excellent member of the team.

When I was a CEO, this was one of the most difficult lessons for me to learn. I felt that it was my job to create an environment where brilliant people of all backgrounds, personality types, and work styles would thrive. And I was right. That was my job. Companies where people with diverse backgrounds and work styles can succeed have significant advantages in recruiting and retaining top talent over those that don't. Still, you can take it too far. And I did.

Here are three examples of the smartest people in the company being the worst employees.

## EXAMPLE 1: THE HERETIC

Any sizable company produces some number of strategies, projects, processes, promotions, and other activities that don't make sense. No large organization achieves perfection. As a result, a company needs lots of smart, super-engaged employees who can identify its particular weaknesses and help it improve them.

However, sometimes a really smart employee develops an agenda other than improving the company. Rather than identifying weaknesses so that he can fix them, he looks for faults to build his case. Specifically, he builds his case that the company is hopeless and run by a bunch of morons. The smarter the employee, the more destructive this type of behavior can be. Simply put, it takes a really smart person to be maximally destructive, because otherwise nobody else will listen to him.

Why would a smart person try to destroy the company that he works for? There are actually many reasons. Here are a few:

1. *She is disempowered.* She feels that she cannot access the people in charge and, as a result, complaining is her only vehicle to get the truth out.

2. *She is fundamentally a rebel.* She will not be happy unless she is rebelling; this can be a deep personality trait. Sometimes these people actually make better CEOs than employees.

3. *She is immature and naive.* She cannot comprehend that the people running the company do not know every minute detail of the operation and therefore they are complicit in everything that's broken.

Often, it's very difficult to turn these kinds of cases around. Once an employee takes a public stance, the social pressure for him to be consistent is enormous. If he tells fifty of his closest friends that the CEO is the stupidest person on the planet, then reversing that position will cost him a great amount of credibility the next time he complains. Most people are not willing to take the hit to their credibility.

## EXAMPLE 2: THE FLAKE

Some brilliant people can be totally unreliable. At Opsware, we once hired an unequivocal genius—Arthur (not his real name) was an engineer in an area of the product where a typical new hire would take three months to become fully productive. Arthur got fully up to speed in two days. On his third day, we gave him a project that was scheduled to take one month. Arthur completed the project in three days with nearly flawless quality. More specifically, he completed the project in seventy-two hours. Seventy-two nonstop hours: No stops, no sleep, no nothing but coding. In his first quarter on the job, he was the best employee that we had and we immediately promoted him.

Then Arthur changed. He would miss days of work without calling in. Then he would miss weeks of work. When he finally showed up, he apologized profusely, but the behavior didn't stop. His work product also degraded. He became sloppy and unfocused. I could not understand how such a stellar employee could go so haywire. His manager wanted to fire him, because the team could no longer count on Arthur for anything. I resisted. I knew that the genius was still in him and I wanted us to find it. We never did. It turned out that Arthur was bipolar and had two significant drug problems: (1) He did not like taking his bipolar medication and (2) he was addicted to cocaine. Ultimately, we had to fire Arthur, but even now, it pains me to think about what might have been.

One need not be bipolar to be a flake, but flaky behavior often has a seriously problematic root cause. Causes range from self-destructive streaks to drug habits to moonlighting for other employers. A company is a team effort and, no matter how high an employee's potential, you cannot get value from him unless he does his work in a manner in which he can be relied upon.

## EXAMPLE 3: THE JERK

This particular smart-bad-employee type can occur anywhere in the organization but is most destructive at the executive level. Most executives can be pricks, dicks, a-holes, or a variety of other profane nouns at times. Being dramatically impolite can be used to improve clarity or emphasize an important lesson. That's not the behavior that I am talking about.

When used consistently, asinine behavior can be crippling. As a company grows, its biggest challenge always becomes communication. Keeping a huge number of people on the same page executing the same goals is never easy. If a member of your staff is a raging jerk, it may be impossible. Some people are so belligerent in their communication style that people just stop talking when they are in the room. If every time anyone brings up an issue with the marketing organization, the VP of marketing jumps down their throats, then guess what topic will never come up? This behavior can become so bad that nobody brings up any topic when the jerk is in the room. As a result, communication across the executive staff breaks down and the entire company slowly degenerates. Note that this only happens if the jerk in question is unquestionably brilliant. Otherwise, nobody will care when she attacks them. The bite only has impact if it comes from a big dog. If one of your big dogs destroys communication on your staff, you need to send her to the pound.

## WHEN DO YOU HOLD THE BUS?

The great football coach John Madden was once asked whether he would tolerate a player like Terrell Owens on his team. Owens was both one of the most talented players in the game and one of the biggest jerks. Madden answered, "If you hold the bus for everyone on the team, then you'll be so late you'll miss the game, so you can't do that.

The bus must leave on time. However, sometimes you'll have a player that's so good that you hold the bus for him, but only him."

Phil Jackson, the coach who has won the most NBA championships, was once asked about his famously flaky superstar Dennis Rodman, "Since Dennis Rodman is allowed to miss practice, does this mean other star players like Michael Jordan and Scottie Pippen can miss practice, too?" Jackson replied, "Of course not. There is only room for one Dennis Rodman on this team. In fact, you really can only have a very few Dennis Rodmans in society as a whole; otherwise, we would degenerate into anarchy."

You may find yourself with an employee who fits one of the above descriptions but nonetheless makes a massive positive contribution to the company. You may decide that you will personally mitigate the employee's negative attributes and keep her from polluting the overall company culture. That's fine, but remember: You can only hold the bus for her.

# OLD PEOPLE

Your startup is going well and as your business expands you hear the dreaded words from someone on your board: "You need to hire some senior people. Some real 'been there, done that' executives to help you get the company to the next level." Really? Is now the time? If so, where do I begin? And once I get them, what do I do with them? And how will I know if they are doing a good job?

The first question you might ask is "Why do I need senior people at all? Won't they just ruin the culture with their fancy clothes, political ambitions, and need to go home to see their families?" To some extent, the answer to all of those may be "yes," which is why this question must be taken quite seriously. However, bringing in the right kind of experience at the right time can mean the difference between bankruptcy and glory.

Let's go back to the first part of the question. Why hire a senior person? The short answer is *time*. As a technology startup, from the day you start until your last breath, you will be in a furious race against time. No technology startup has a long shelf life. Even the best ideas become terrible ideas after a certain age. How would Facebook go if Zuckerberg started it last week? At Netscape, we went public when we were fifteen months old. Had we started six months later, we would have been late to a market with thirty-seven other browser companies. Even if nobody beats you to the punch, no matter how beautiful your dream most employees will lose faith after the first five or six years of not achieving it. Hiring someone who has already done what you are trying to do can radically speed up your time to success.

But CEO, beware: Hiring senior people into a startup is kind of like an athlete taking performance-enhancing drugs. If all goes well, you will achieve incredible new heights. If all goes wrong, you will start degenerating from the inside out.

In order to make all go well, if you are considering hiring a senior person do not chase an abstract rationale like "adult supervision" or "becoming a real company." A weak definition of what you are looking for will lead to a bad outcome. The proper reason to hire a senior person is *to acquire knowledge and experience in a specific area.*

For example, as a technical founder, you probably do not have terrific knowledge of how to build a worldwide sales channel, how to create an invincible brand, or how to identify and negotiate ecosystem-altering business development deals. Acquiring a world-class senior person can dramatically accelerate your company's ability to succeed in these areas.

One good test for determining whether to go with outside experience versus internal promotion is to figure out whether you value inside knowledge or outside knowledge more for the position. For example, for engineering managers the comprehensive knowledge of the code base and engineering team is usually more important and difficult to acquire than knowledge of how to run scalable engineering organizations. As a result, you might very well value the knowledge of your own organization more than that of the outside world.

In hiring someone to sell your product to large enterprises, the opposite is true. Knowing how your target customers think and operate, knowing their cultural tendencies, understanding how to recruit and measure the right people in the right regions of the world to maximize your sales—these things turn out to be far more valuable than knowing your own company's product and culture. This is why when the head of engineering gets promoted from within, she often succeeds. When the head of sales gets promoted from within, she almost always fails. Asking yourself, "Do I value internal or external knowledge more for this position?" will help you determine whether to go for experience or youth.

## ONCE THEY ARRIVE

Bringing senior people on board can be fraught with peril, as I have outlined in the sections "Why It's Hard to Bring Big Company Execs into Little Companies" and "Hiring Executives: If You've Never Done the Job, How Do You Hire Somebody Good?" (see pages 119 and 124).

Equally difficult is managing them effectively once they come on board. Senior people pose several important challenges:

- *They come with their own culture.* They will bring the habits, the communication style, and values from the company they grew up in. It's very unlikely these will match your environment exactly.

- *They will know how to work the system.* Because senior people come from larger environments, they usually develop the skills to navigate and be effective in those environments. These skills may seem political and unusual in your environment.

- *You don't know the job as well as they do.* In fact, you are hiring them precisely because you don't know how to do the job. So how do you hold them accountable for doing a good job?

In order to prevent the internal degeneration mentioned earlier, it's important to be aware of the above issues and then employ appropriate countermeasures to make sure they don't metastasize.

First, you should demand cultural compliance. It's fine that people come from other company cultures. It's true that some of those cultures will have properties that are superior to your own. But this is your company, your culture, and your way of doing business. Do not be intimidated by experience on this issue; stick to your guns and stick to your culture. If you want to expand your culture to incorporate some of the new thinking, that's fine, but do so explicitly—do not drift. Next, watch for politically motivated tactics and do not tolerate them.

Perhaps most important, set a high and clear standard for performance. If you want to have a world-class company, you must make sure that the people on your staff—be they young or old—are world-class. It is not nearly enough that someone on your staff can do the job better than you can, because you are incompetent at the job—that's why you hired them in the first place.

Be careful not to set a low bar because you have not done the work to know what good is. For example, I've seen many a young CEO excited about her company's competency in marketing and PR because she got a bunch of positive stories on her launch. That's not a high PR standard. Anybody can get reporters to write nice things about a sweet, cuddly baby of a company. Only world-class PR people can deal with gangly, pimple-ridden, teenage companies. World-class PR people can turn around negative stories. World-class PR people can turn chicken shit into chicken salad. Turning chicken shit into chicken salad requires long-term, trusted relationships, deep know-how, and the confidence to make use of both appropriately. PR kids don't have any of the three.

One excellent way to develop a high standard is to interview people who you see doing a great job in their field. Find out what their standard is and add it to your own. Once you determine a high yet achievable performance bar, hold your executive to that high standard even if you have no idea how they might achieve it. It's not your job to figure out how to create an incredible brand, tilt the playing field by cutting a transformational deal, or achieve a sales goal that nobody thought possible—that's what you are paying them to do. That's why you hired them.

Finally, you'll need your new executive to be more than just a goal achiever. She will need to be well rounded and part of the team. Bill Campbell developed an excellent methodology for measuring executives in a balanced way that will help you achieve this. He breaks performance down into four distinct areas:

1. **Results against objectives** Once you've set a high standard, it will be straightforward to measure your executive against that standard.

2. **Management** Even if an executive does a superb job achieving her goals, that doesn't mean she is building a strong and loyal team. It's important to understand how well she is managing, even if she is hitting her goals.

3. **Innovation** It's quite possible for an executive to hit her goal for the quarter by ignoring the future. For example, a great way for an engineering manager to hit her goals for features and dates is by building a horrible architecture, which won't even support the next release. This is why you must look beyond the black-box results and into the sausage factory to see how things get made.

4. **Working with peers** This may not be intuitive at first, but executives must be effective at communicating, supporting, and getting what they need from the other people on your staff. Evaluate them along this dimension.

## AW, MAN, YOU SOLD YOUR SOUL

Hiring the first senior people into your company may feel like selling your soul, and if you are not careful, you may well end up selling the soul of your company. But if you want to make something from nothing, you have to take risks and you have to win your race against time. This means acquiring the very best talent, knowledge, and experience even if it requires dealing with some serious age diversity.

# ONE-ON-ONE

After I first wrote about one-on-ones, people flooded me with feedback about one-on-ones. About half the responders chastised me, saying that one-on-ones were useless and that I shouldn't put so much emphasis on them. The other half wanted to know how to run more effective one-on-ones. It seems to me that both groups are likely talking about two sides of the same coin.

Perhaps the CEO's most important operational responsibility is designing and implementing the communication architecture for her company. The architecture might include the organizational design, meetings, processes, email, yammer, and even one-on-one meetings with managers and employees. Absent a well-designed communication architecture, information and ideas will stagnate, and your company will degenerate into a bad place to work. While it is quite possible to design a great communication architecture without one-on-one meetings, in most cases one-on-ones provide an excellent mechanism for information and ideas to flow up the organization and should be part of your design.

Generally, people who think one-on-one meetings are a bad idea have been victims of poorly designed ones. The key to a good one-on-one meeting is the understanding that it is the *employee's* meeting rather than the manager's meeting. This is the free-form meeting for all the pressing issues, brilliant ideas, and chronic frustrations that do not fit neatly into status reports, email, and other less personal and intimate mechanisms.

If you are an employee, how do you get feedback from your manager on an exciting but only 20 percent formed idea that you're not sure is relevant, without sounding like a fool? How do you point out that a colleague you do not know how to work with is blocking your progress without throwing her under the bus? How do you get help when you love your job but your personal life is melting down? Through a status report? On email? Yammer? Asana? Really? For these and other important areas of discussions, one-on-ones can be essential.

If you like structured agendas, then the employee should set the agenda. A good practice is to have the employee send you the agenda in advance. This will give her a chance to cancel the meeting if nothing is pressing. It also makes clear that it is her meeting and will take as much or as little time as she needs. During the meeting, since it's the employee's meeting, the manager should do 10 percent of the talking and 90 percent of the listening. Note that this is the opposite of most one-on-ones.

While it's not the manager's job to set the agenda or do the talking, the manager should try to draw the key issues out of the employee. The more introverted the employee, the more important this becomes. If you manage engineers, drawing out issues will be an important skill to master.

Some questions that I've found to be very effective in one-on-ones:

- If we could improve in any way, how would we do it?

- What's the number-one problem with our organization? Why?

- What's not fun about working here?

- Who is really kicking ass in the company? Whom do you admire?

- If you were me, what changes would you make?

- What don't you like about the product?

- What's the biggest opportunity that we're missing out on?

- What are we not doing that we should be doing?

- Are you happy working here?

In the end, the most important thing is that the best ideas, the biggest problems, and the most intense employee life issues make their way to the people who can deal with them. One-on-ones are a time-tested way to do that, but if you have a better one, go ahead with your bad self.

# PROGRAMMING YOUR CULTURE

Ask ten founders about company culture and what it means and you'll get ten different answers. It's about office design, it's about screening out the wrong kinds of employees, it's about values, it's about fun, it's about alignment, it's about finding like-minded employees, it's about being cultlike.

So what is culture? Does culture matter? If so, how much time should you spend on it?

Let's start with the second question first. The primary thing that any technology startup must do is build a product that's at least ten times better at doing something than the current prevailing way of doing that thing. Two or three times better will not be good enough to get people to switch to the new thing fast enough or in large enough volume to matter. The second thing that any technology startup must do is to *take the market*. If it's possible to do something ten times better, it's also possible that you won't be the only company to figure that out. Therefore, you must take the market before somebody else does. Very few products are ten times better than the competition's, so unseating the *new* incumbent is much more difficult than unseating the old one.

If you fail to do both of those things, your culture won't matter one bit. The world is full of bankrupt companies with world-class cultures. Culture does not make a company.

So, why bother with culture at all? Three reasons:

1. It matters to the extent that it can help you achieve the above goals.

2. As your company grows, culture can help you preserve your key values, make your company a better place to work, and help it perform better in the future.

3. Perhaps most important, after you and your people go through the inhuman amount of work that it will take to build a successful company, it will be an epic tragedy if your company culture is such that even you don't want to work there.

## CREATING A COMPANY CULTURE

When I refer to company culture, I am not referring to other important activities like company values and employee satisfaction. Specifically, I am writing about designing a way of working that will:

- Distinguish you from competitors

- Ensure that critical operating values persist such as *delighting customers* or *making beautiful products*

- Help you identify employees who fit with your mission

Culture means lots of other things in other contexts, but the above will be plenty to discuss here.

When you start implementing your culture, keep in mind that most of what will be retrospectively referred to as your company's culture will not have been designed into the system, but rather will have evolved over time based on your behavior and the behavior of your early employees. As a result, you will want to focus on a small number of cultural design points that will influence a large number of behaviors over a long period of time.

In his bestselling book *Built to Last,* Jim Collins wrote that one of the things that long-lasting companies he studied have in common is a "cult-like culture." I found this description to be confusing because it seems to imply that as long as your culture is weird enough and you are rabid enough about it, you will succeed on the cultural front.

That's related to the truth, but not actually true. In reality, Collins was right that a properly designed culture often ends up looking cultlike in retrospect, but that's not the initial design principle. You needn't think hard about how you can make your company seem bizarre to outsiders. However, you do need to think about how you can be provocative enough to change what people do every day.

Ideally, a cultural design point will be trivial to implement but have far-reaching behavioral consequences. Key to this kind of mechanism is shock value. If you put something into your culture that is so disturbing that it always creates a conversation, it will change behavior. As we learned in *The Godfather,* ask a Hollywood mogul to give someone a job and he might not respond. Put a horse's head in his bed and unemployment will drop by one. Shock is a great mechanism for behavioral change.

Here are three examples:

**Desks made out of doors** Very early on, Jeff Bezos, founder and CEO of Amazon.com, envisioned a company that made money by delivering value *to* rather than extracting value *from* its customers. In order to do that, he wanted to be both the price leader and customer service leader for the long run. You can't do that if you waste a lot of money. Jeff could have spent years auditing every expense and raining hell on anybody who overspent, but he decided to build frugality into his culture. He did it with an incredibly simple mechanism: All desks at Amazon.com for all time would be built by buying cheap doors from Home Depot and nailing legs to them. These door desks are not great ergonomically, nor do they fit with Amazon.com's $150 billion–plus market capitalization, but when a shocked new employee asks why she must work on a makeshift desk constructed out of random Home Depot parts, the answer comes back with withering consistency: "We look for every opportunity to save money so that we can deliver the best products for the lowest cost." If you don't like sitting at a door, then you won't last long at Amazon.

**Ten dollars per minute** When we started Andreessen Horowitz, Marc and I wanted the firm to treat entrepreneurs with great respect. We remembered how psychologically brutal the process of building a company was. We wanted the firm to respect the fact that in the bacon-and-egg breakfast of a startup, we were with the chicken and the entrepreneur was the pig: We were involved, but she was committed. We thought that one way to communicate respect would be to always be on time to meetings with entrepreneurs. Rather than make them wait in our lobby for thirty minutes while we attended to more important business like so many venture capitalists that we visited, we wanted our people to be on time, prepared, and focused. Unfortunately, anyone who has ever worked anywhere knows that this is easier said than done. In order to shock the company into the right behavior, we instituted a ruthlessly enforced ten-dollar-per-minute fine for being late to a meeting with an entrepreneur. So, for example: You are on a really important call and will be ten minutes late? No problem, just bring one hundred dollars to the meeting and pay your fine. When new employees come on board, they find this shocking, which gives us a great opportunity to explain in detail why we respect entrepreneurs. If you don't think entrepreneurs are more important than venture capitalists, we can't use you at Andreessen Horowitz.

**Move fast and break things** Mark Zuckerberg believes in innovation and he believes there can be no great innovation without great risk. So, in the early days of Facebook, he deployed a shocking motto: *Move fast and break things*. Did the CEO really want us to break things? I mean, he's telling us to break things! A motto that shocking forces everyone to stop and think. When they think, they realize that if you move fast and innovate, you will break things. If you ask yourself, "Should I attempt this breakthrough? It will be awesome, but it may cause problems in the short term," you have your answer. If you'd rather be right than innovative, you won't fit in at Facebook.

Prior to figuring out the exact form of your company's shock therapy, be sure that your mechanism agrees with your values. For example, Jack Dorsey will never make his own desks out of doors at Square because at Square, beautiful design trumps frugality. When you walk into Square, you can feel how seriously they take design.

## WHY DOGS AT WORK
## AND YOGA AREN'T CULTURE

Startups today do all kinds of things to distinguish themselves. Many great, many original, many quirky, but most of them will not define the company's culture. Yes, yoga may make your company a better place to work for people who like yoga. It may also be a great team-building exercise for people who like yoga. Nonetheless, it's not culture. It will not establish a core value that drives the business and helps promote it in perpetuity. It is not specific with respect to what your business aims to achieve. Yoga is a perk.

Somebody keeping a pit bull in her cube may be shocking. The lesson learned—that animal lovers are welcome or that employees can live however they want—may provide some societal value, but it does not connect to your business in a distinguishing way. Every smart company values its employees. Perks are good, but they are not culture.

## THE POINT OF IT ALL

In the later section "How to Evaluate CEOs" (see page 235), I describe the CEO job as knowing what to do and getting the company to do what you want. Designing a proper company culture will help you get your company to do what you want in certain important areas for a very long time.

# TAKING THE MYSTERY OUT OF SCALING A COMPANY

If you want to build an important company, then at some point you have to scale. People in startup land often talk about the magic of how few people built the original Google or the original Facebook, but today's Google employs twenty thousand people and today's Facebook employs more than fifteen hundred people. So, if you want to do something that matters, then you are going to have to learn the black art of scaling a human organization.

Often board members give entrepreneurs two bits of advice regarding scale:

1. Get a mentor.

2. Find some "been there, done that" executives who already know how to scale.

These answers, while fine as far as they go, have some important limitations. First, if you don't know anything about scaling an organization, then it will be very difficult for you to evaluate people for that job. Imagine trying to find a killer engineer if you'd never written a single program. Second, many investor-board members don't know anything about scaling a company, either, and can be suckers for people who have the experience but not the skills. If you've ever worked in a large organization, you know that there are plenty of people with experience running them but none of the requisite skills to run them well.

This advice is still good, but the right way to pick both the best mentors and best employees is by first learning the basics; then you can apply the myriad of scaling techniques in the management literature depending on the context.

## THE BASIC IDEA: GIVE GROUND GRUDGINGLY

When an organization grows in size, things that were previously easy become difficult. Specifically, the following things that cause no trouble when you are small become big challenges as you grow:

- Communication

- Common knowledge

- Decision making

In order to get a clear understanding of the problem, let's start with the boundary condition. Imagine a company of one employee. That employee writes and tests all the code, does all the marketing and sales, and manages herself. She has complete knowledge of everything in the company, makes all the decisions, needn't communicate with anyone, and is totally aligned with herself. As the company grows, things will only get worse in each dimension.

On the other hand, if the company doesn't expand, then it will never be much of a company, so the challenge is to grow but degrade as slowly as possible.

There is a great analogue to this concept in American football. An offensive lineman's job is to protect the quarterback from onrushing defensive linemen. If the offensive lineman attempts to do this by holding his ground, the defensive lineman will easily run around him and crush the quarterback. As a result, offensive linemen are taught to lose the battle slowly or *to give ground grudgingly*. They are taught to back up and allow the defensive lineman to advance, but just a little at a time.

When you scale an organization, you will also need to give ground grudgingly. Specialization, organizational structure, and process all complicate things and implementing them will feel like you are moving away from common knowledge and quality communication. It is very much like the offensive lineman taking a step backward. You will lose ground, but you will prevent your company from descending into chaos.

## HOW TO DO IT

At the point when adding people into the company feels like more work than the work that you can offload to the new employees, the defensive lineman has run around you and you probably need to start giving ground grudgingly.

## SPECIALIZATION

The first scale technique to implement is specialization. In startups, everybody starts out as a jack-of-all-trades. For example, engineers write code, manage the build system, test the product, and, increasingly, deploy it and operate it. This works well in the beginning because everybody knows everything and the need to communicate is minimized; there are no complicated handoffs, because there is nobody to hand anything to. As the company grows, it becomes increasingly difficult to add new engineers, because the learning curve starts to get super-steep. Getting a new engineer up to speed starts to become more difficult than doing the work yourself. At this point, you need to specialize.

By dedicating people and teams to such tasks as the build environment, the test environment, and operations, you will create some complexity—handoffs across groups, potentially conflicting agendas, and specialized rather than common knowledge. In order to mitigate these issues, you will need to consider other scale techniques like *organizational design* and *process.*

## ORGANIZATIONAL DESIGN

The first rule of organizational design is that all organizational designs are bad. With any design, you will optimize communication among some parts of the organization at the expense of other parts. For example, if you put product management in the engineering organization, you will optimize communication between product management and engineering at the expense of communication between product management and marketing. As a result, as soon as you roll out the new organization, people will find fault with it and they will be right.

Nonetheless, at some point the monolithic design of one huge organization runs out of gas and you will need to split things into smaller subgroups. At the most basic level, you'll want to consider giving the groups that you've specialized their own managers as they grow. You may want a QA manager, for example. After that, things become more complex. Do client engineering and server engineering have their own groups or do you organize by use cases and include all technical components? When you get really big, you'll need to decide whether to organize the entire company around functions (for example, sales, marketing, product management, engineering) or around missions—self-contained business units that contain multiple functions.

Your goal is to choose the least of all evils. Think of the organizational design as the communications architecture for your company. If you want people to communicate, the best way to accomplish that is to make them report to the same manager. By contrast, the further

away people are in the organizational chart, the less they will communicate. The organizational design is also the architecture for how
the company communicates with the outside world. For example, you
might want to organize your sales force by product to maximize communication with the relevant product groups and maximize the product competency of the sales force. If you do that, then you will do so
at the expense of simplicity for customers who buy multiple products
and will now have to deal with multiple salespeople.

With this in mind, here are the basic steps to organizational design:

1. *Figure out what needs to be communicated.* Start by listing
   the most important knowledge and who needs to have it.
   For example, knowledge of the product architecture must
   be understood by engineering, QA, product management,
   marketing, and sales.

2. *Figure out what needs to be decided.* Consider the types of
   decisions that must get made on a frequent basis: feature
   selection, architectural decisions, how to resolve support
   issues. How can you design the organization to put the maximum number of decisions under the domain of a designated
   manager?

3. *Prioritize the most important communication and decision paths.* Is it more important for product managers to
   understand the product architecture or the market? Is it
   more important for engineers to understand the customer
   or the architecture? Keep in mind that these priorities will
   be based on today's situation. If the situation changes, then
   you can reorganize.

4. *Decide who's going to run each group.* Notice that this is
   the fourth step, not the first. You want to optimize the organization for the people—for the people doing the work—
   not for the managers. Most large mistakes in organizational

design come from putting the individual ambitions of the people at the top of the organization ahead of the communication paths for the people at the bottom of the organization. Making this step four will upset your managers, but they will get over it.

5. *Identify the paths that you did not optimize.* As important as picking the communication paths that you will optimize is identifying the ones that you will not. Just because you deprioritized them doesn't mean they are unimportant. If you ignore them entirely, they will surely come back to bite you.

6. *Build a plan for mitigating the issues identified in step five.* Once you've identified the likely issues, you will know the processes you will need to build to patch the impending cross-organizational challenges.

These six steps should get you pretty far. When we examine advanced organizational design, we'll also need to consider trade-offs such as speed versus cost, how to roll out organizational changes, and how often you should reorganize.

## PROCESS

The purpose of process is communication. If there are five people in your company, you don't need process, because you can just talk to each other. You can hand off tasks with a perfect understanding of what's expected, you pass important information from one person to another, and you can maintain high-quality transactions with no bureaucratic overhead. With four thousand people, communication becomes more difficult. Ad hoc, point-to-point communication no longer works. You need something more robust—a communication bus or, to use the conventional term for human communication buses, a process.

A process is a formal, well-structured communication vehicle. It can be a heavily engineered Six Sigma process or it can be a well-structured regular meeting. The size of the process should be scaled up or down to meet the needs of the communication challenge that it facilitates.

When communication in an organization spans across organizational boundaries, processes will help ensure that the communication happens and that it happens with quality. If you are looking for the first process to implement in your company, consider the interview process. It usually runs across organizational boundaries (the hiring group, human resources—or wherever the recruiter lives, and supporting groups), involves people from outside the company (the candidate), and is critically important to the success of the company.

Who should design a process? The people who are already doing the work in an ad hoc manner. They know what needs to be communicated and to whom. Naturally they will be the right group to formalize the existing process and make it scalable.

When should you start implementing processes? While that varies depending on your situation, keep in mind that it's much easier to add new people to old processes than new processes to old people. Formalize what you are doing to make it easy to onboard new people.

Much has been written about process design, so I won't repeat that here. I have found the "The Basics of Production," the first chapter of Andy Grove's *High Output Management*, to be particularly helpful. For new companies, here are a few things to keep in mind:

- *Focus on the output first.* What should the process produce? In the case of the interview process, an outstanding employee. If that's the goal, what's the process to get there?

- *Figure out how you'll know if you are getting what you want at each step.* Are you getting enough candidates? Are

you getting the right candidates? Will your interview process find the right person for the job? Once you select the
person, will they accept the job? Once they accept the job,
will they become productive? Once they become productive, will they stay with your company? How will you measure each step?

- *Engineer accountability into the system.* Which organization and which individual is responsible for each step? What
  can you do to increase the visibility of their performance?

## FINAL THOUGHT

The process of scaling a company is not unlike the process of scaling
a product. Different sizes of company impose different requirements
on the company's architecture. If you address those requirements too
early, your company will seem heavy and sluggish. If you address
those requirements too late, your company may melt down under the
pressure. Be mindful of your company's true growth rate as you add
architectural components. It's good to anticipate growth, but it's bad
to overanticipate growth.

# THE SCALE ANTICIPATION
# FALLACY

The other day I was talking to a couple of friends of mine, one a VC and the other a CEO. During the meeting, we discussed one of the executives at the CEO's company. The executive in question performs exceptionally but lacks experience managing at larger scale. My friend the VC innocently advised the CEO to carefully consider whether the executive would scale to meet the company's needs in the future. I responded swiftly, aggressively, and loudly, saying, "That's a horrible idea and makes no sense at all." Both of my friends were startled at my outburst. Normally I am disciplined enough to refrain from letting my feelings pass straight through my mouth without stopping at my brain for review. Why the outburst? Here is my answer.

As CEO, you must constantly evaluate all the members of your team. However, evaluating people against the future needs of the company based on a theoretical view of how they will perform is counterproductive, for the following reasons:

- *Managing at scale is a learned skill rather than a natural ability.* Nobody comes out of the womb knowing how to manage a thousand people. Everybody learns at some point.

- *It's nearly impossible to make the judgment in advance.* How do you tell in advance if an executive can scale? Was it obvious that Bill Gates would learn how to scale when he was a Harvard dropout? How do you go about making that decision?

- *The act of judging people in advance will retard their development.* If you make a judgment that someone is incapable of doing something such as running a larger organization, will it make sense to teach them those skills or even point out the anticipated deficiencies? Probably not. You've already decided they can't do it.

- *Hiring scalable execs too early is a bad mistake.* There is no such thing as a great executive. There is only a great executive for a specific company at a specific point in time. Mark Zuckerberg is a phenomenal CEO for Facebook. He would not be a good CEO for Oracle. Similarly, Larry Ellison does a terrific job at Oracle but he would not be the right person to manage Facebook. If you judge your team in advance and have a high sense of urgency, you will bring in executives who can manage at high scale in advance of needing them. Unfortunately, you will probably ignore their ability to do the job for the next twelve months, which is the only relevant measure. As a result, you will swap out good executives for worse ones.

- *You still have to make the judgment at the actual point in time when you hit the higher level of scale.* Even if you avoid the trap of hiring a scalable executive too early or retarding the new executive's development, you still haven't actually bought yourself anything by making the prejudgment. Regardless of what you decided at point in time A, you still have to evaluate the situation with far better data at point in time B.

- *It's no way to live your life or run an organization.* Deciding (with woefully incomplete data) that someone who works their butt off, does a terrific job, and loyally contributes to your mission won't be with you three years from now takes you to a dark place. It's a place of information hiding, dishonesty, and stilted communication. It's a place where prejudice substitutes for judgment. It's a place where judgment replaces teaching. It's a place where teamwork becomes internal warfare. Don't go there.

So, if you don't prejudge people's ability to scale, how do you make the judgment? You should evaluate your team at least once a quarter on all dimensions. Two keys can help you avoid the scale anticipation trap:

- *Don't separate scale from the rest of the evaluation.* The relevant question isn't whether an executive can scale; it's whether the executive can do the job at the current scale. You should evaluate holistically and this will prevent you from separating out scale, which often leads to an unwise prediction of future performance.

- *Make the judgment on a relative rather than an absolute scale.* Asking yourself whether an executive is great can be extremely difficult to answer. A better question: For this company at this exact point in time, does there exist an executive who I can hire who will be better? If my biggest competitor hires that person, how will that impact our ability to win?

Predicting whether an executive can scale corrupts your ability to manage, is unfair, and doesn't work.

# CHAPTER 7

# HOW TO LEAD EVEN WHEN YOU DON'T KNOW WHERE YOU ARE GOING

"This for every ghetto in the hood
Nas the Don, Super Cat the Don Dada, understood."

—NAS, "THE DON"

After selling the Loudcloud business to EDS, we immediately plunged into a new crisis. Our investors could not understand how selling all of our revenue and all of our customers could possibly leave us with anything worth investing in. As a result, institutional investors sold all of their Opsware shares, and our stock price fell to $0.35 per share. This turned out to be a noteworthy price, because it computed to a market capitalization equal to half of the cash we had in the bank. This signaled that investors believed that the Opsware business had no value, and they further expected us to burn up half our cash before coming to our senses and returning the cash to investors. To make matters more miserable, I received a notice from NASDAQ informing me that if I did not get our stock price above $1 within the next ninety days, they would delist us and we would trade with the penny stocks.

I brought this cheery news to the board with three options:

1. *Reverse split.* We could reverse split the stock 10:1 and have ten times fewer shares and a ten times higher stock price.

2. *Give in.* We could become a penny stock.

3. *Hit the road.* I could go on the road and try to get enough people to buy so that the stock price would triple.

The board was extremely sympathetic and open to every option. Andy Rachleff pointed out that the negative connotation with reverse splits among investors had lessened due to the sheer number of them. Marc hypothesized that being delisted in a post-newspaper economy might not matter so much.

Still, I did not want to reverse split the stock. More than anything, it felt like a capitulation and a dramatic sign of weakness. Reverse splitting would say to the market that I believed we really were worth half the cash that we had in the bank. I also didn't want the company to get delisted. I knew that Marc would be right one day, but I also knew that many institutional investors were prohibited from buying penny stocks in the current day and age. I decided to hit the road.

The first big question was "Hit the road to go see whom?" At that time, most institutional investors wouldn't invest in stocks with prices under $10, let alone under $1. So Marc and I called our networking guru, the famous angel investor Ron Conway, for advice. We told him the story, explaining that the $20 million a year EDS contract alone made the Opsware business worth something, and adding that we had a great team and huge amount of intellectual property, so there was no reason for us to trade at half of cash. Ron listened carefully and then said, "I think you should go see Herb Allen."

I had heard about Herb's investment bank, Allen & Company, but didn't really know much about him. Allen & Company was famous for running the best business conference in the world. The conference is invitation-only and consistently attracts guests whom you will never find at any other conference. People like Bill Gates, Warren Buffett, and Rupert Murdoch are regulars. Allen & Company may attract more top-tier guests than all other business conferences combined—it's that good.

Marc and I arrived at the Allen & Company office in Manhattan, located in the Coca-Cola building where Herb's father, Herbert, had served on the board of directors for many years. If a single word could describe the Allen & Company office it would be *classy*. Beautifully decorated, yet not flashy, the office was both elegant and comfortable.

Like his office, Herb himself was both unassuming and classy. He opened the meeting by complimenting Ron, saying that any referral from Ron was personally important to him. Marc and I then carefully took Herb through the story of Loudcloud—how we had sold the services business to EDS, retaining the software and the key people, and had secured a $20 million a year software license. Beyond that, we had a totally clean balance sheet and were surely worth more than $0.35 per share. Herb listened attentively to the entire presentation and then said, "I'd like to be helpful. I'll see what I can do." I had no idea if he meant, as many in Silicon Valley would mean, "Screw off, I'm not buying a penny stock" or if he meant what he'd said. I soon found out.

Over the next couple of months, Allen & Company bought Opsware stock, Herb Allen personally bought Opsware stock, and several Allen & Company clients became major investors. This activity propelled the stock from $0.35 to $3 per share in a matter of months. We'd avoided delisting, rebuilt the shareholder base, and given employees hope. Everything was largely due to a single meeting with Herb Allen.

Years later I asked Herb why he believed in our company at a time when nobody else did. I pointed out that, at the time, Allen & Company wasn't very involved in technology, let alone data center automation. Herb replied, "I didn't understand anything about your business and I understood very little about your industry. What I saw was two guys come visit me when every other public company CEO and chairman was hiding under their desk. Not only did you come see me, but you were more determined and convinced you would succeed than guys running giant businesses. Investing in courage and determination was an easy decision for me."

That's how Herb Allen does business. And that's why, if given the chance, you'd be a fool not to do business with Herb.

Perhaps the most important thing that I learned as an entrepreneur was to focus on what I needed to get right and stop worrying about all the things that I did wrong or might do wrong. This section encapsulates the various parts of those lessons and provides guidance on how to get the important things right.

# THE MOST DIFFICULT CEO SKILL

By far the most difficult skill I learned as CEO was the ability to manage my own psychology. Organizational design, process design, metrics, hiring, and firing were all relatively straightforward skills to master compared with keeping my mind in check. I thought I was tough going into it, but I wasn't tough. I was soft.

Over the years, I've spoken to hundreds of CEOs, all with the same experience. Nonetheless, very few people talk about it and I have never read anything on the topic. It's like the fight club of management: The first rule of the CEO psychological meltdown is don't talk about the psychological meltdown.

At the risk of violating the sacred rule, I will attempt to describe the condition and prescribe some techniques that helped me. In the end, this is the most personal and important battle that any CEO will face.

## IF I'M DOING A GOOD JOB,
## WHY DO I FEEL SO BAD?

Generally, someone doesn't become a CEO unless she has a high sense of purpose and cares deeply about the work she does. In addition, a CEO must be accomplished enough or smart enough that people will want to work for her. Nobody sets out to be a bad CEO, run a dysfunctional organization, or create a massive bureaucracy that grinds her company to a screeching halt. Yet no CEO ever has a smooth path to a great company. Along the way, many things go wrong and all of them could have and should have been avoided.

The first problem is that everybody learns to be a CEO by being a CEO. No training as a manager, general manager, or in any other job actually prepares you to run a company. The only thing that prepares you to run a company is running a company. This means that you will face a broad set of things that you don't know how to do that require skills you don't have. Nevertheless, everybody will expect you to know how to do them, because, well, you are the CEO. I remember when I first became CEO, an investor asked me to send him the "cap table." I had a vague idea of what he meant, but I didn't actually know what the format was supposed to look like or what should be included or excluded. It was a silly little thing and I had much bigger things to worry about, but everything is hard when you don't actually know what you are doing. I wasted quite a bit of time sweating over that stupid spreadsheet.

Even if you know what you are doing, things go wrong. Things go wrong because building a multifaceted human organization to compete and win in a dynamic, highly competitive market turns out to be really hard. If CEOs were graded on a curve, the mean on the test would be 22 out of 100. This kind of mean can be psychologically challenging for a straight-A student. It is particularly challenging because nobody tells you that the mean is 22.

If you manage a team of ten people, it's quite possible to do so with very few mistakes or bad behaviors. If you manage an organization of one thousand people, it is quite impossible. At a certain size, your company will do things that are so bad that you never imagined that you'd be associated with that kind of incompetence. Seeing people fritter away money, waste each other's time, and do sloppy work can make you feel bad. If you are the CEO, it may well make you sick.

And to rub salt into the wound and make matters worse, it's your fault.

## NOBODY TO BLAME

*"You can't blame Jazz musicians*
*or David Stern with his NBA fashion issues."*
—NAS, "HIP HOP IS DEAD"

When people in my company would complain about one thing or another being broken, such as the expense reporting process, I would joke that it was all my fault. The joke was funny, because it wasn't really a joke. Every problem in the company was indeed my fault. As the founding CEO, every hire and every decision that the company ever made happened under my direction. Unlike a hired gun who comes in and blames all of the problems on the prior regime, there was literally nobody for me to blame.

If someone was promoted for all the wrong reasons, that was my fault. If we missed the quarterly earnings target, that was my fault. If a great engineer quit, that was my fault. If the sales team made unreasonable demands on the product organization, that was my fault. If the product had too many bugs, that was my fault. It kind of sucked to be me.

Being responsible for everything and getting a 22 on the test starts to weigh on your consciousness.

## TOO MUCH BROKEN STUFF

Given this stress, CEOs often make one of the following two mistakes:

1. They take things too personally.

2. They do not take things personally enough.

In the first scenario, the CEO takes every issue incredibly seriously and personally and urgently moves to fix it. Given the volume of the issues, this motion usually results in one of two scenarios. If the CEO is outwardly focused, she ends up terrorizing the team to the point where nobody wants to work at the company anymore. If the CEO is inwardly focused, she ends up feeling so sick from all the problems that she can barely make it to work in the morning.

In the second scenario, in order to dampen the pain of the rolling disaster that is the company, the CEO takes a Pollyannaish attitude: It's not so bad. In this view, none of the problems is actually that bad and they needn't be dealt with urgently. By rationalizing away the issues, the CEO feels better about herself. The problem is that she doesn't actually fix any of the problems and the employees eventually become quite frustrated that the chief executive keeps ignoring the most basic problems and conflicts. Ultimately, the company turns to crap.

Ideally, the CEO will be urgent yet not insane. She will move aggressively and decisively without feeling emotionally culpable. If she can separate the importance of the issues from how she feels about them, she will avoid demonizing her employees or herself.

## IT'S A LONELY JOB

In your darkest moments as CEO, discussing fundamental questions about the viability of your company with your employees can have obvious negative consequences. On the other hand, talking to your board and outside advisers can be fruitless. The knowledge gap between you and them is so vast that you cannot actually bring them fully up to speed in a manner that's useful in making the decision. You are all alone.

At Loudcloud, when the dot-com bubble burst and subsequently sent most of our customers into bankruptcy, it crippled our business and devastated our balance sheet. Or rather, that was one interpretation. Another interpretation, and necessarily the official story for the company, was that we still had plenty of money in the bank and were signing up traditional enterprise customers at an impressive rate. Which interpretation was closer to the truth? In the absence of someone to talk to, that's a question that I asked myself about three thousand times. (As an aside, asking oneself anything three thousand times turns out to be a bad idea.) In this case, I had two specific difficult questions:

1. What if the official interpretation was wrong? What if I was misleading everyone from investors to employees? In that case, I should be removed from my position immediately.

2. What if the official interpretation was right? What if I was grinding my brain into sawdust for no reason at all? What if I was taking the company off track by questioning my own direction? In that case, I should be removed from my position immediately.

As is usually the case, there was no way to know which interpretation was right until much later. It turned out that neither was actually right. The new customers didn't save us, but we figured out another way to survive and ultimately succeed. The key to getting to the right outcome was to keep from getting married to either the positive or the dark narrative.

My friend Jason Rosenthal took over as CEO of Ning in 2010. As soon as he became CEO, he faced a cash crisis and had to choose among three difficult choices: (1) radically reduce the size of the company, (2) sell the company, or (3) raise money in a highly dilutive way. Think about those choices:

1. Lay off a large set of talented employees whom he worked very hard to recruit and, as a result, likely severely damage the morale of the remaining people.

2. Sell out all of the employees whom he had been working side by side with for the past several years (Jason was promoted into the position) by selling the company without giving them a chance to perform or fulfill their mission.

3. Drastically reduce the ownership position of the employees and make their hard work economically meaningless.

Choices like these cause migraine headaches. Tip to aspiring entrepreneurs: If you don't like choosing between horrible and cataclysmic, don't become CEO.

Jason sought advice from some of the best minds in the industry, but ultimately he was completely alone in the final decision. Nobody had the answer and whatever the answer, Jason was the one who had to live with the consequences. So far his decision to reduce staff by letting go of primarily the most recent hires has paid off. Revenue at Ning is soaring and team morale is high. If it had gone worse (or ultimately goes bad), it would be all Jason's fault and it would be up to Jason to find a new answer. Whenever I see Jason, I like to say, "Welcome to the show." Jason eventually sold Ning to Glam and went on to become CEO of Lytro.

At times like this, it's important to understand that nearly every company goes through life-threatening moments. My partner at Andreessen Horowitz, Scott Weiss, relayed that it's so common that there is an acronym for it, WFIO, which stands for "We're Fucked, It's Over" (it's pronounced "whiff-ee-yo"). As he describes it, every company goes through at least two and up to five of these episodes (although I'm pretty sure that I went through at least a dozen at Opsware). In all cases, WFIOs feel much worse than they are—especially for the CEO.

## TECHNIQUES TO CALM YOUR NERVES

The problem with psychology is that everybody's is different. With that as a caveat, over the years I developed a few techniques for dealing with myself. I hope you find them useful, too.

*Make some friends.* Although it's nearly impossible to get high-quality advice on the tough decisions that you make, it is extremely useful from a psychological perspective to talk to people who have been through similarly challenging decisions.

*Get it out of your head and onto paper.* When I had to explain to my board that, since we were a public company, I thought that it would be best if we sold all of our customers and all of our revenue and changed business, it was messing with my mind. In order to finalize that decision, I wrote down a detailed explanation of my logic. The process of writing that document separated me from my own psychology and enabled me to make the decision swiftly.

*Focus on the road, not the wall.* When someone learns to drive a race car, one of the first lessons taught is that when you are going around a curve at 200 mph, do not focus on the wall; focus on the road. If you focus on the wall, you will drive right into it. If you focus on the road, you will follow the road. Running a company is like that. There are always a thousand things that can go wrong and sink the ship. If you focus too much on them, you will drive yourself nuts and likely crash your company. Focus on where you are going rather than on what you hope to avoid.

## DON'T PUNK OUT AND DON'T QUIT

As CEO, there will be many times when you feel like quitting. I have seen CEOs try to cope with the stress by drinking heavily, checking out, and even quitting. In each case, the CEO has a marvelous rationalization about why it was okay for him to punk out or quit, but none of them will ever be great CEOs.

Great CEOs face the pain. They deal with the sleepless nights, the cold sweats, and what my friend the great Alfred Chuang (legendary cofounder and CEO of BEA Systems) calls "the torture." Whenever I meet a successful CEO, I ask them how they did it. Mediocre CEOs point to their brilliant strategic moves or their intuitive business sense or a variety of other self-congratulatory explanations. The great CEOs tend to be remarkably consistent in their answers. They all say, "I didn't quit."

# THE FINE LINE BETWEEN
# FEAR AND COURAGE

"I tell my kids, what is the difference between a hero and a coward? What is the difference between being yellow and being brave? No difference. Only what you do. They both feel the same. They both fear dying and getting hurt. The man who is yellow refuses to face up to what he's got to face. The hero is more disciplined and he fights those feelings off and he does what he has to do. But they both feel the same, the hero and the coward. People who watch you judge you on what you do, not how you feel."

—CUS D'AMATO, LEGENDARY BOXING TRAINER

When my partners and I meet with entrepreneurs, the two key characteristics that we look for are brilliance and courage. In my experience as CEO, I found that the most important decisions tested my courage far more than my intelligence.

The right decision is often obvious, but the pressure to make the wrong decision can be overwhelming. It starts with small things.

When founders come in to pitch our firm—one as the CEO and the other as president—the conversation often goes like this:

"Who is running the company?"

"We are," they both say.

"Who makes the final decision?"

"We do."

"How long do you expect to run that way?"

"Forever."

"So you've decided to make it more difficult for every employee to get work done so that you don't have to decide who is in charge, is that right?"

That usually results in silence.

Intellectually, it should be clear that it is easier for employees to go to one decision maker than two. It's not really very complicated at all. Unfortunately, the clear and present social pressure often overwhelms the long-term benefits of organizing the company properly. Because the founders do not have the courage to decide who is in charge, every employee suffers the inconvenience of double approval.

More important, decisions only get scarier as a company grows. When we decided to take Loudcloud public with only $2 million in revenue, it was not a hard choice intellectually—the alternative was to go bankrupt. It was nonetheless terrifying to do something that most employees, everyone in the press, and many investors thought was nuts.

## WHEN MAKING THE RIGHT CHOICE
## REQUIRES INTELLIGENCE AND COURAGE

Sometimes the decision itself is rather complicated, which makes the courage challenge even more difficult. CEOs possess a different set of data, knowledge, and perspective than anybody else in the company. Frequently, some of the employees and board members are more experienced and more intelligent than the CEO. The only reason the CEO can make a better decision is her superior knowledge.

To make matters worse, when a CEO faces a particularly difficult decision, she may have only a slight preference for one choice over another—say 54 percent kill a product line, 46 percent keep it. If the really smart people on the board and on her staff take the other side, her courage will be severely tested. How can she kill the product when she is not even sure if she is making the right decision and everyone is against her? If she's wrong, she will have been wrong in the face of advice from her top advisers. If she is right, will anybody even know?

Recently, a large company offered to buy one of our portfolio companies. The deal was lucrative and compelling given the portfolio company's progress to date and revenue level. The founder/CEO (I'll call him Hamlet—not his real name) thought that selling did not make sense due to the giant market opportunity that he was pursuing, but he still wanted to make sure that he made the best possible choice for investors and employees. Hamlet wanted to reject the offer, but only marginally. To complicate matters, most of the management team and the board thought the opposite. It did not help that the board and the management team were far more experienced than Hamlet. As a result, Hamlet spent many sleepless nights worrying about whether he was right. He realized that it was impossible to know. This did not help him sleep. In the end, Hamlet made the best and most courageous decision he could and did not sell the company. I believe that will prove to be the defining moment of his career.

Interestingly, as soon as Hamlet made the decision, the entire board and executive team immediately embraced the choice. Why? If they wanted to sell the company enough to advise the CEO to give up his dream, how could they reverse themselves so quickly? It turns out that the most important data point driving their earlier preference for selling the company was Hamlet's initial ambivalence—the team supported the decision they *thought* the CEO wanted. Hamlet did not realize this and interpreted their desire to sell to be the result of a thorough analysis. Luckily for everybody involved, he had the courage to make the right decision.

The general problem can be seen in the social credit matrix below. The expected social rewards for making the crowd-influenced decision appear better than those for making the decision you think is right:

|  | You are right | You are wrong |
|---|---|---|
| **You decide against the crowd.** | Few remember that you made the decision, but the company succeeds. | Everybody remembers the decision and you are downgraded, ostracized, or fired. |
| **You decide with the crowd.** | Everyone who advised you remembers the decision and the company succeeds. | You receive the minimum blame possible for getting it wrong, but the company suffers. |

On the surface, it appears that if the decision is a close call, it's much safer to go with the crowd. In reality, if you fall into this trap, the crowd will influence your thinking and make a 70-30 decision seem like a 51-49 decision. This is why courage is critical.

## COURAGE, LIKE CHARACTER, CAN BE DEVELOPED

In all the difficult decisions that I made through the course of running Loudcloud and Opsware, I never once felt brave. In fact, I often felt scared to death. I never lost those feelings, but after much practice I learned to ignore them. That learning process might also be called the *courage development process.*

In life, everybody faces choices between doing what's popular, easy, and wrong versus doing what's lonely, difficult, and right. These decisions intensify when you run a company, because the consequences get magnified a thousandfold. As in life, the excuses for CEOs making the wrong choice are always plentiful.

| Life Excuse | CEO Excuse |
|---|---|
| Other smart people made the same mistake. | It was a close call. |
| All my friends wanted to do it. | The team was against me and I couldn't go against the team. |
| All the cool kids are doing it. | It was industry best practice; I didn't realize it was illegal. |
| It wasn't perfect, so I decided not to compete. | We never achieved total product-market fit, so we never tried to sell our product. |

Every time you make the hard, correct decision you become a bit more courageous and every time you make the easy, wrong decision you become a bit more cowardly. If you are CEO, these choices will lead to a courageous or cowardly company.

## LAST THOUGHT

Over the past ten years, technological advances have dramatically lowered the financial bar for starting a new company, but the courage bar for building a great company remains as high as it has ever been.

# ONES AND TWOS

Jim Collins, in his bestselling book *Good to Great*, demonstrates through massive research and comprehensive analysis that when it comes to CEO succession, internal candidates dramatically outperform external candidates. The core reason is knowledge. Knowledge of technology, prior decisions, culture, personnel, and more tends to be far more difficult to acquire than the skills required to manage a larger organization. Collins does not, however, explain why internal candidates sometimes fail as well. I will attempt to do so here. I will focus the discussion on two core skills for running an organization: First, knowing what to do. Second, getting the company to do what you know. While being a great CEO requires both skills, most CEOs tend to be more comfortable with one or the other. I call managers who are happier setting the direction of the company *Ones* and those who more enjoy making the company perform at the highest level *Twos*.

## WHAT ONES LIKE AND DON'T LIKE

Ones like spending most of their time gathering information from a broad variety of sources, from employees to customers to competitors. Ones love making decisions. Although they prefer to have comprehensive information when they make a decision, they comfortably make decisions with very little information when necessary. Ones have great strategic minds and enjoy nothing more than a good game of eight-dimensional chess against their best competitors.

Ones sometimes get bored with many of the important execution details required to run a company, such as process design, goal setting, structured accountability, training, and performance management.

Most founding CEOs tend to be Ones. When founding CEOs fail, a significant reason is that they never invested the time to be competent enough in the Two tasks to direct those activities effectively. The resulting companies become too chaotic to reach their full potential and the CEO ends up being replaced.

## WHAT TWOS LIKE AND DON'T LIKE

Twos, on the other hand, thoroughly enjoy the process of making the company run well. They insist upon super-clear goals and strongly prefer not to change goals or direction unless absolutely necessary.

Twos like to participate in strategic discussions but often have difficulty with the strategic thinking process itself. Where a One might be perfectly comfortable spending one day a week reading, studying, and thinking, doing so would make a Two very nervous, because it would not feel like work to them. A Two would get antsy at the thought of all the processes that might be improved, people who might be held accountable to achieving the standard, or sales calls that could be made while he was wasting time just thinking about strategy.

Big decisions worry Twos much more than they worry Ones. Circumstances often force both Ones and Twos to make critical decisions with insufficient data, but Ones generally feel fine about doing that and do not get overly anxious about the consequences. Twos, by contrast, can become highly agitated about such things and sometimes overcomplicate the decision-making process in order to provide a false feeling of thoroughness about the choice.

CEOs who are Twos, despite their love of action, can sometimes bring decision making in a company to a halt.

## YOU NEED BOTH CHARACTERISTICS
## TO BE A GOOD CEO

While people tend to be Ones or Twos, with discipline and hard work natural Twos can be competent at One tasks and Ones can be competent at Two tasks. If a CEO ignores the dimension of management she doesn't like, she generally fails. Ones end up in chaos and Twos fail to pivot when necessary.

## FUNCTIONAL ONES

Often Two executives act as Ones for their functions, but Twos as members of the executive team. For example, the head of sales might easily make all the decisions that are local to the sales organization but prefer to take direction with respect to the overall company plans. This is the best kind of multilayer leadership possible, because directions are clear and decisions are made rapidly with precision.

## HOW ORGANIZATIONS TEND
## TO BE CONSTRUCTED

The primary purpose of the organizational hierarchy in a company is decision-making efficiency. It follows that most CEOs tend to be Ones. If the person at the top of the decision-making hierarchy doesn't like making extremely complex decisions, the company's processes will be slow and unwieldy.

If you're a One, it can be counterproductive to have another One on your staff, because she will want to set her own direction rather than follow yours. This kind of strategic contention can confuse the organization and send employees in opposing directions. As a result, many great One CEOs employ primarily Twos and Functional Ones on their staff.

## WHAT HAPPENS AT SUCCESSION?

This brings us to the question of succession. Since most organizations are run by Ones and have a team of Twos (sometimes Functional Ones) reporting to them, replacing the CEO can be extremely tricky. Do you promote someone from the executive staff even though they are likely a Two? Microsoft did this in 2000 when they replaced Bill Gates, a prototypical One, with Steve Ballmer, literally his number two. Or do you reach deep into the organization and pull a One from a level lower where they are likely to exist? General Electric famously did this with Jack Welch in 1981. It was an incredibly bold move by GE—not only did they promote an executive two levels down in the organizational chart past all of his superiors, but in doing so they named the youngest CEO in the history of GE. It's difficult for most board members to even conceive of the possibility that there is a One deep in the organization who is more qualified to run the company than anyone on the executive staff.

Both methods can be problematic. The first approach leaves the company in the charge of a Two. As the company faces forks in the road, decision making may slow down and the company may lose its edge. In addition, the natural Ones (in Microsoft's case, stellar executives such as Paul Maritz and Brad Silverberg) will eventually leave.

In scenario two, by promoting someone past everyone on the executive team and making them CEO (as GE did), you will likely cause massive turnover of the executive staff. In fact, in very short order, almost none of the original GE executives remained under Welch. In a diversified conglomerate like GE, this kind of rough transition is possible. For companies in the highly dynamic technology business, the super-high-turnover scenario is more dangerous.

## THE BIG CONCLUSION

The big conclusion will be a big disappointment for those looking for an answer. The answer is there is no easy answer. CEO transition is hard. If you bring people in from the outside, you lower your chances for success. If you promote from within, you must deal with the One-Two phenomenon. Ideally, you'll promote a One and the rest of the executive team will be glad you did. Too bad things are rarely ideal.

# FOLLOW THE LEADER

There is no prototype for the perfect CEO. Radically different styles—think Steve Jobs, Bill Campbell, and Andy Grove—can all lead to great outcomes. Perhaps the most important attribute required to be a successful CEO is leadership. So what is leadership and how do we think about it in the context of the CEO job? Are great leaders born or made?

Most people define leadership in the same way that Supreme Court justice Potter Stewart famously defined pornography when he said, "I know it when I see it." For our purposes, we can generalize this to be the measure of the quality of a leader: the quantity, quality, and diversity of people who want to follow her.

So what makes people want to follow a leader? We look for three key traits:

- The ability to articulate the vision

- The right kind of ambition

- The ability to achieve the vision

Let's take these in order.

## THE ABILITY TO ARTICULATE THE VISION:
## THE STEVE JOBS ATTRIBUTE

Can the leader articulate a vision that's interesting, dynamic, and compelling? More important, can the leader do this when things fall apart? More specifically, when the company gets to a point when it does not make financial sense for any employee to continue working there, will the leader be able to articulate a vision that's compelling enough to make people stay?

I believe Jobs's greatest achievement as a visionary leader was in getting so many super-talented people to continue following him at NeXT, long after the company lost its patina, and in getting the employees of Apple to buy into his vision when the company was weeks away from bankruptcy. It's difficult to imagine any other leader being so compelling that he could accomplish these goals back-to-back, and this is why we call this one the Steve Jobs attribute.

## THE RIGHT KIND OF AMBITION: THE BILL
## CAMPBELL ATTRIBUTE

One of the biggest misperceptions in our society is that a prerequisite for becoming a CEO is to be selfish, ruthless, and callous. In fact, the opposite is true and the reason is obvious. The first thing that any successful CEO must do is get really great people to work for her. Smart people do not want to work for people who do not have their interests in mind and in heart.

Most of us have experienced this in our careers: a bright, ambitious, hardworking executive whom nobody good wants to work for and who, as a result, delivers performance far worse than one might imagine.

Truly great leaders create an environment where the employees feel that the CEO cares more about the employees than she cares about herself. In this kind of environment, an amazing thing happens:

A huge number of employees believe it's *their* company and behave accordingly. As the company grows large, these employees become quality control for the entire organization. They set the work standard that all future employees must live up to. As in, "Hey, you need to do a better job on that data sheet—you are screwing up my company."

I call this characteristic the Bill Campbell attribute after the man who is the best I've ever seen at this. If you talk to people who worked in any of the many organizations that Bill has run, they refer to those organizations as "my organization" or "my company." A huge part of why he has been so remarkably strong in this dimension of leadership is that he's completely authentic. He would happily sacrifice his own economics, fame, glory, and rewards for his employees. When you talk to Bill, you get the feeling that he cares deeply about you and what you have to say, because he does. And all of that shows up in his actions and follow-through.

## THE ABILITY TO ACHIEVE THE VISION: THE ANDY GROVE ATTRIBUTE

The final leg of our leadership stool is competence, pure and simple. If I buy into the vision and believe that the leader cares about me, do I think she can actually achieve the vision? Will I follow her into the jungle with no map forward or back and trust that she will get me out of there?

I like to refer to this as the Andy Grove attribute. Andy Grove will always be my model of CEO competence. He earned a Ph.D. in electrical engineering, wrote the best management book I've ever read (*High Output Management*), and tirelessly refined his craft. Not only did he write exceptional books on management, but he taught management classes at Intel throughout his tenure.

In his classic book *Only the Paranoid Survive*, Grove tells how he led Intel through the dramatic transition from the memory business to the microprocessor business. In making that change he walked away from nearly all his revenue. He humbly credits others in the company with coming to the strategic conclusion before he did, but the credit for swiftly and successfully leading the company through the transition goes to Dr. Grove. Changing your primary business as a sixteen-year-old large, public company raises a lot of questions.

Andy describes an incident with one of his employees: "One of them attacked me aggressively, asking, 'Does it mean that you can conceive of Intel without being in the memory business?' I swallowed hard and said, 'Yes, I guess I can.' All hell broke loose."

Despite shocking many of his best employees with this radical strategy, ultimately the company trusted Andy. They trusted him to rebuild their company around an entirely new business. That trust turned out to be very well placed.

## SO, ARE GREAT LEADERS BORN OR MADE?

Let's look at this one attribute at a time:

- **Articulating the vision** There is no question that some people are much better storytellers than others. However, it is also true that anybody can greatly improve in this area through focus and hard work. All CEOs should work on the vision component of leadership.

- **Alignment of interests** I am not sure if the Bill Campbell attribute is impossible to learn, but I am pretty sure that it is impossible to teach. Of the three, this one most fits the bill "born not made."

- **Ability to achieve the vision** This attribute can absolutely be learned; perhaps this is why Andy Grove's tolerance for incompetence was legendarily low. Indeed, the enemy of competence is sometimes confidence. A CEO should never be so confident that she stops improving her skills.

In the end, some attributes of leadership can be improved more than others, but every CEO should work on all three. Furthermore, each attribute enhances all three. If people trust you, they will listen to your vision even if it is less articulate. If you are super-competent, they will trust you and listen to you. If you can paint a brilliant vision, people will be patient with you as you learn the CEO skills and give you more leeway with respect to their interests.

# PEACETIME CEO/WARTIME CEO

Bill Campbell always used to say to me, "Ben, you're the best CEO that I work with." This always seemed crazy to me, because he was working with Steve Jobs, Jeff Bezos, and Eric Schmidt at the time while my company was going straight into the wall. One day I called him on it and said, "Bill, why would you say that? Do results not count?" He said, "There are lots of good peacetime CEOs and lots of good wartime CEOs, but almost no CEOs that can function in both peacetime and in wartime. You're a peacetime/wartime CEO."

By my calculation, I was a peacetime CEO for three days and wartime CEO for eight years. I still have a hard time shaking the wartime flashbacks. I'm not the only one who has experienced this. Dennis Crowley, the founder of Foursquare, told me that he thinks about this tension—between wartime and peacetime—every day. The same goes for a lot of tech companies.

For instance, when Eric Schmidt stepped down as CEO of Google and founder Larry Page took over, much of the news coverage focused on Page's ability to be the "face of Google" since Page is far more shy and introverted than the gregarious and articulate Schmidt. While an interesting issue, this analysis misses the main point. Schmidt was much more than Google's front man; as Google's *peacetime* chief executive, he led the greatest technology business expansion in the last ten years. Larry Page, in contrast, seems to have determined that Google is moving into war and he clearly intends to be a *wartime* CEO. This has been a profound change for Google and the entire high-tech industry.

## DEFINITIONS AND EXAMPLES

Peacetime in business means those times when a company has a large advantage over the competition in its core market, and its market is growing. In times of peace, the company can focus on expanding the market and reinforcing the company's strengths.

In wartime, a company is fending off an imminent existential threat. Such a threat can come from a wide range of sources, including competition, dramatic macroeconomic change, market change, supply chain change, and so forth. The great wartime CEO Andy Grove marvelously describes the forces that can take a company from peacetime to wartime in his book *Only the Paranoid Survive.*

A classic peacetime mission is Google's effort to make the Internet faster. Google's position in the search market is so dominant that they determined that anything that makes the Internet faster accrues to their benefit since it enables users to do more searches. As the clear market leader, they focus more on expanding the market than dealing with their search competitors. In contrast, a classic wartime mission was Andy Grove's drive to get out of the memory business in the mid-1980s due to an irrepressible threat from the Japanese semiconductor companies. In this mission, the competitive threat—which could have bankrupted the company—was so great that Intel had to exit its core business, which employed 80 percent of its staff.

My greatest management discovery through the transition was that peacetime and wartime require radically different management styles. Interestingly, most management books describe peacetime CEO techniques and very few describe wartime. For example, a basic principle in most management books is that you should never embarrass an employee in a public setting. On the other hand, in a room filled with people, Andy Grove once said to an employee who entered the meeting late, "All I have in this world is time, and you are wasting my time." Why such different approaches to management?

In peacetime, leaders must maximize and broaden the current opportunity. As a result, peacetime leaders employ techniques to encourage broad-based creativity and contribution across a diverse set of possible objectives. In wartime, by contrast, the company typically has a single bullet in the chamber and must, at all costs, hit the target. The company's survival in wartime depends upon strict adherence and alignment to the mission.

When Steve Jobs returned to Apple, the company was weeks away from bankruptcy—a classic wartime scenario. He needed everyone to move with precision and follow his exact plan; there was no room for individual creativity outside the core mission. In stark contrast, as Google achieved dominance in the search market, Google's management fostered peacetime innovation by enabling and even requiring every employee to spend 20 percent of their time on their own new projects.

Peacetime and wartime management techniques can both be highly effective when employed in the right situations, but they are very different. The peacetime CEO does not resemble the wartime CEO.

## PEACETIME CEO/WARTIME CEO

Peacetime CEO knows that proper protocol leads to winning. Wartime CEO violates protocol in order to win.

Peacetime CEO focuses on the big picture and empowers her people to make detailed decisions. Wartime CEO cares about a speck of dust on a gnat's ass if it interferes with the prime directive.

Peacetime CEO builds scalable, high-volume recruiting machines. Wartime CEO does that, but also builds HR organizations that can execute layoffs.

Peacetime CEO spends time defining the culture. Wartime CEO lets the war define the culture.

Peacetime CEO always has a contingency plan. Wartime CEO knows that sometimes you gotta roll a hard six.

Peacetime CEO knows what to do with a big advantage. Wartime CEO is paranoid.

Peacetime CEO strives not to use profanity. Wartime CEO sometimes uses profanity purposefully.

Peacetime CEO thinks of the competition as other ships in a big ocean that may never engage. Wartime CEO thinks the competition is sneaking into her house and trying to kidnap her children.

Peacetime CEO aims to expand the market. Wartime CEO aims to win the market.

Peacetime CEO strives to tolerate deviations from the plan when coupled with effort and creativity. Wartime CEO is completely intolerant.

Peacetime CEO does not raise her voice. Wartime CEO rarely speaks in a normal tone.

Peacetime CEO works to minimize conflict. Wartime CEO heightens the contradictions.

Peacetime CEO strives for broad-based buy-in. Wartime CEO neither indulges consensus building nor tolerates disagreements.

Peacetime CEO sets big, hairy, audacious goals. Wartime CEO is too busy fighting the enemy to read management books written by consultants who have never managed a fruit stand.

Peacetime CEO trains her employees to ensure satisfaction and career development. Wartime CEO trains her employees so they don't get their asses shot off in the battle.

Peacetime CEO has rules like "We're going to exit all businesses where we're not number one or two." Wartime CEO often has no businesses that are number one or two and therefore does not have the luxury of following that rule.

## CAN A CEO BE BOTH?

Can a CEO build the skill sets to lead in both peacetime and wartime?

One could easily argue that I failed as a peacetime CEO but succeeded as a wartime one. John Chambers had a great run as peacetime CEO of Cisco but has struggled as Cisco has moved into war with Juniper, HP, and a range of new competitors. Steve Jobs, who employed a classical wartime management style, removed himself as CEO of Apple in the 1980s during their longest period of peace before coming back to Apple for a spectacular run more than a decade later, during their most intense war period.

I believe that the answer is yes, but it's hard. Mastering both wartime and peacetime skill sets means understanding the many rules of management and knowing when to follow them and when to violate them.

Be aware that management books tend to be written by management consultants who study successful companies during their times of peace. As a result, the resulting books describe the methods of peacetime CEOs. In fact, other than the books written by Andy Grove, I don't know of any management books that teach you how to manage in wartime like Steve Jobs or Andy Grove.

## BACK TO THE BEGINNING

It turned out that a little wartime was just what the doctor ordered for Google. Page's precise and exacting leadership has led to brilliant execution in integrating identity across Google's broad product line, from the rise of Android to brilliant new products like Google Glass. Sometimes you need to go to war.

# MAKING YOURSELF A CEO

The other day, a friend of mine asked me whether CEOs were born or made. I said, "That's kind of like asking if Jolly Ranchers are grown or made. CEO is an unnatural job." The surprised look on his face made me realize that perhaps it wasn't as obvious as I'd originally thought.

Most people actually assume the opposite—CEOs are born, not made. I often listen as other venture capitalists and board members rapidly evaluate a founder and conclude that she's not "CEO material." I am not sure how they figure these things out so fast. It generally takes years for a founder to develop the CEO skill set and it is usually extremely difficult for me to tell whether she will make it.

In athletics, some things, like becoming a sprinter, can be learned relatively quickly because they start with a natural motion and refine it. Others, like boxing, take much longer to master because they require lots of unnatural motions and lots of specific technique. For example, as I mentioned earlier, when going backward in boxing it's critically important to pick up your back foot first, because if you get hit while walking backward the natural way—picking up your front foot first—it often leads to getting knocked cold. Learning to make this unnatural motion feel natural takes a great deal of practice. If you do what feels most natural as a CEO, you may also get knocked cold.

Being CEO requires lots of unnatural motion. From an evolution-ary standpoint, it is natural to do things that make people like you. It enhances your chances for survival. Yet to be a good CEO, in order to be liked in the long run, you must do many things that will upset people in the short run. Unnatural things.

Even the most basic CEO building blocks will feel unnatural at first. If your buddy tells you a funny story, it would feel quite weird to evaluate her performance. It would be totally unnatural to say, "Gee, I thought that story really sucked. It had potential, but you were un-derwhelming on the buildup and then you totally flubbed the punch line. I suggest that you go back, rework it, and present it to me again tomorrow."

Doing so would be quite bizarre, but evaluating people's perfor-mances and constantly giving feedback is precisely what a CEO must do. If she doesn't, the more complex motions such as writing reviews, taking away territory, handling politics, setting compensation, and firing people will be either impossible or handled rather poorly.

Giving feedback turns out to be the unnatural atomic building block atop which the unnatural skill set of management gets built. But how does one master the unnatural?

## THE SHIT SANDWICH

A popular and sometimes effective technique for feedback beginners is something that experienced managers call the *Shit Sandwich*. The technique is marvelously described in the classic management text *The One Minute Manager*. The basic idea is that people open up to feedback far more if you start by complimenting them (slice of bread number one), then you give them the difficult message (the shit), then wrap up by reminding them how much you value their strengths (slice of bread number two). The shit sandwich also has the positive side effect of focusing the feedback on the behavior rather than the person, because you establish up front that you really value the person. This is a key concept in giving feedback.

The shit sandwich can work well with junior employees but has the following challenges:

- It tends to be overly formal. Because you have to preplan and script the sandwich to make it come out correctly, the process can feel formal and judgmental to the employee.

- After you do it a couple of times, it will lack authenticity. The employee will think, "Oh boy, she's complimenting me again. I know what's coming next, the shit."

- More senior executives will recognize the shit sandwich immediately and it will have an instant negative effect.

Early in my career, I attempted to deliver a carefully crafted shit sandwich to a senior employee and she looked at me like I was a little kid and said, "Spare me the compliment, Ben, and just tell me what I did wrong." At that point, I thought that I was definitely not born to be a CEO.

## THE KEYS

To become elite at giving feedback, you must elevate yourself beyond a basic technique like the shit sandwich. You must develop a style that matches your own personality and values. Here are the keys to being effective:

- *Be authentic.* It's extremely important that you believe in the feedback that you give and not say anything to manipulate the recipient's feelings. You can't fake the funk.

- *Come from the right place.* It's important that you give people feedback because you want them to succeed and not because you want them to fail. If you really want someone to succeed, then make her feel it. Make her feel you. If she feels you and you are in her corner, then she will listen to you.

■ *Don't get personal.* If you decide to fire somebody, fire her. Don't prepare her to get fired. Prepare her to succeed. If she doesn't take the feedback, that's a different conversation.

■ *Don't clown people in front of their peers.* While it's okay to give certain kinds of feedback in a group setting, you should strive never to embarrass someone in front of their peers. If you do so, then your feedback will have little impact other than to cause the employee to be horribly ashamed and to hate your guts.

■ *Feedback is not one-size-fits-all.* Everybody is different. Some employees are extremely sensitive to feedback while others have particularly thick skin and often thick skulls. Stylistically, your tone should match the employee's personality, not your mood.

■ *Be direct, but not mean.* Don't be obtuse. If you think somebody's presentation sucks, don't say, "It's really good, but could use one more pass to tighten up the conclusion." While it may seem harsh, it's much better to say, "I couldn't follow it and I didn't understand your point and here are the reasons why." Watered-down feedback can be worse than no feedback at all because it's deceptive and confusing to the recipient. But don't beat them up or attempt to show your superiority. Doing so will defeat your purpose because when done properly, feedback is a dialogue, not a monologue.

## FEEDBACK IS A DIALOGUE,
## NOT A MONOLOGUE

You may be the CEO and you may be telling somebody about something that you don't like or disagree with, but that doesn't mean you're right. Your employee should know more about her function than you. She should have more data than you. You may be wrong.

As a result, your goal should be for your feedback to open up rather than close down discussion. Encourage people to challenge your judgment and argue the point to conclusion. Culturally, you want high standards thoroughly discussed. You want to apply tremendous pressure to get the highest-quality thinking yet be open enough to find out when you are wrong.

## HIGH-FREQUENCY FEEDBACK

Once you've mastered the keys, you should practice what you've mastered all the time. As CEO, you should have an opinion on absolutely everything. You should have an opinion on every forecast, every product plan, every presentation, and even every comment. Let people know what you think. If you like someone's comment, give her the feedback. If you disagree, give her the feedback. Say what you think. Express yourself.

This will have two critically important positive effects:

- *Feedback won't be personal in your company.* If the CEO constantly gives feedback, then everyone she interacts with will just get used to it. Nobody will think, "Gee, what did she really mean by that comment? Does she not like me?" Everybody will naturally focus on the issues, not an implicit random performance evaluation.

- *People will become comfortable discussing bad news.* If people get comfortable talking about what *each other* are doing wrong, then it will be very easy to talk about what *the company* is doing wrong. High-quality company cultures get their cue from data networking routing protocols: Bad news travels fast and good news travels slowly. Low-quality company cultures take on the personality of the Wicked Witch of the West in *The Wiz*: "Don't nobody bring me no bad news."

## MAKING THE CEO

Being CEO also requires a broad set of more advanced skills, but the key to reaching the advanced level and feeling like you were born to be CEO is mastering the unnatural.

If you are a founder CEO and you feel awkward or incompetent when doing some of these things and believe there is no way that you'll be able to do it when your company is one hundred or one thousand people, welcome to the club. That's exactly how I felt. So did every CEO I've ever met. This is the process. This is how you get made.

# HOW TO EVALUATE CEOS

No position in a company is more important than the CEO and, as a result, no job gets more scrutiny. The job is so poorly defined that you can end up doing all kinds of nutty things (especially if you listen to some people who say things like "the CEO should be the number-one salesperson").

Sadly, little of this analysis that's been done benefits CEOs, since most of the discussions happen behind their backs. Here I want to take a step in the opposite direction. By describing how I evaluate CEOs, I am at the same time describing what I think the job of the CEO is. Here are the key questions we ask:

1. Does the CEO know what to do?

2. Can the CEO get the company to do what she knows?

3. Did the CEO achieve the desired results against an appropriate set of objectives?

## 1. DOES THE CEO KNOW WHAT TO DO?

One should interpret this question as broadly as possible. Does the CEO know what to do in all matters all the time? This includes matters of personnel, financing, product strategy, goal sizing, and marketing. At a macro level, does the CEO set the right strategy for the company and know its implications in every detail of the company?

I evaluate two distinct facets of knowing what to do:

- **Strategy** In good companies, the *story* and the *strategy* are the same thing. As a result, the proper output of all the strategic work is *the story*.

- **Decision making** At the detailed level, the output of *knowing what to do* is *the speed and quality of the CEO's decisions*.

### The strategy and the story

The CEO must set the context within which every employee operates. The context gives meaning to the specific work that people do, aligns interests, enables decision making, and provides motivation. Well-structured goals and objectives contribute to the context, but they do not provide the whole story. More to the point, they are not *the story*. The story of the company goes beyond quarterly or annual goals and gets to the hard-core question of *why*. *Why* should I join this company? *Why* should I be excited to work here? *Why* should I buy its product? *Why* should I invest in the company? *Why* is the world better off as a result of this company's existence?

When a company clearly articulates its story, the context for everyone—employees, partners, customers, investors, and the press—becomes clear. When a company fails to tell its story, you hear phrases like

- These reporters don't get it.

- Who is responsible for the strategy in this company?

- We have great technology, but need marketing help.

The CEO doesn't have to be the creator of the vision. Nor does she have to be the creator of the story. But she must be the keeper of the vision and the story. As such, the CEO ensures that the company story is clear and compelling.

The story is not the mission statement; the story does not have to be succinct. It is the story. Companies can take as long as they need to tell it, but they must tell it and it must be compelling. A company without a story is usually a company without a strategy.

Want to see a great company story? Read Jeff Bezos's three-page letter he wrote to shareholders in 1997. In telling Amazon's story in this extended form—not as a mission statement, not as a tagline—Jeff got all the people who mattered on the same page as to what Amazon was about.

### Decision making

Some employees make products, some make sales; the CEO makes decisions. Therefore, a CEO can most accurately be measured by the speed and quality of those decisions. Great decisions come from CEOs who display an elite mixture of intelligence, logic, and courage.

As already noted, courage is particularly important, because every decision that a CEO makes is based on incomplete information. At the time of any given decision, the CEO will generally have less than 10 percent of the information typically present in the post hoc Harvard Business School case study. As a result, the CEO must have the courage to bet the company on a direction even though she does not know if the direction is right. The most difficult decisions (and often the most important) are difficult precisely because they will be deeply unpopular with the CEO's most important constituencies (employees, investors, and customers).

The best decision that I made in my career—to sell the Loudcloud business to EDS and become Opsware—would have lost by a landslide had I put it to a vote with my employees, my investors, or my customers.

As CEO, there is never enough time to gather all information needed to make a decision. You must make hundreds of decisions big and small in the course of a typical week. You cannot simply stop all other activities to gather comprehensive data and do exhaustive analysis to make that single decision. Knowing this, you must continuously and systematically gather knowledge in the company's day-to-day activities so that you will have as much information as possible when the decision point arrives.

In order to prepare to make any decision, you must systematically acquire the knowledge of everything that might impact any decision that you might make. Questions such as:

- What are the competitors likely to do?

- What's possible technically and in what time frame?

- What are the true capabilities of the organization and how can you maximize them?

- How much financial risk does this imply?

- What will the issues be, given your current product architecture?

- Will the employees be energized or despondent about this promotion?

Great CEOs build exceptional strategies for gathering the required information continuously. They embed their quest for intelligence into all of their daily actions from staff meetings to customer meetings to one-on-ones. Winning strategies are built on comprehensive knowledge gathered in every interaction the CEO has with an employee, a customer, a partner, or an investor.

## 2. CAN THE CEO GET THE COMPANY TO DO WHAT SHE KNOWS?

If the CEO paints a compelling vision and makes fast, high-quality decisions, can she then get the company to execute her vision? The first ingredient in being able to do this is leadership, as I outlined in the section "Follow the Leader."

In addition, executing well requires a broad set of operational skills. The larger the organization, the more elaborate the requisite skill set.

In order for a company to execute a broad set of decisions and initiatives, it must:

- **Have the capacity to do so.** In other words, the company must contain the necessary talent in the right positions to execute the strategy.

- **Be a place where every employee can get things accomplished.** The employees must be motivated, communication must be strong, the amount of common knowledge must be vast, and the context must be clear.

### Is the CEO building a world-class team?

The CEO is responsible for the executive team plus the fundamental interview and hiring processes for all employees. She must make sure the company sources the best candidates and the screening processes yield the candidates with the right combination of talent and skills. Ensuring the quality of the team is a core part of running the company. Great CEOs constantly assess whether they are building the best team.

The output of this capability is the quality of the team. It's important to note that team quality is tightly tied to the specific needs of the company in the challenges it faces at the point in time it faces them. As a result, it's quite possible that the executive team changes several times, but the team is high quality the entire way and there is no attrition problem.

### Is it easy for employees to contribute to the mission?

The second part of the evaluation determines whether the CEO can effectively run the company. To test this, I like to ask this question: "How easy is it for any given individual contributor to get her job done?"

In well-run organizations, people can focus on their work (as opposed to politics and bureaucratic procedures) and have confidence that if they get their work done, good things will happen both for the company and for them personally. By contrast, in a poorly run organization, people spend much of their time fighting organizational boundaries and broken processes.

While it may be quite easy to describe, building a well-run organization requires a high level of skill. The skills required range from organizational design to performance management. They involve the incentive structure and the communication architecture that drive and enable every individual employee. When a CEO "fails to scale," it's usually along this dimension. In practice, very few CEOs get an A on this particular test.

Netflix's CEO, Reed Hastings, put great effort into designing a system that enables employees to be maximally effective. His presentation of this design is called Reference Guide on Our Freedom and Responsibility Culture. It walks through what Netflix values in their employees, how they screen for those values during the interview process, how they reinforce those values, and how they scale this system as the number of employees grows.

### 3. DID THE CEO ACHIEVE THE DESIRED RESULTS AGAINST AN APPROPRIATE SET OF OBJECTIVES?

When measuring results against objectives, start by making sure the objectives are correct. CEOs who excel at board management can "succeed" by setting objectives artificially low. Great CEOs who fail to pay attention to board management can "fail" by setting objectives too high. Early in a company's development, objectives can be particularly misleading since nobody really knows the true size of the opportunity. Therefore, the first task in accurately measuring results is setting objectives correctly.

I also try to keep in mind that the size and nature of the opportunity varies quite a bit across companies. Hoping that a hardware company can be as capital-light as a consumer Internet company or trying to get Yelp to grow as fast as Twitter doesn't make sense and can be quite destructive. CEOs should be evaluated against their company's opportunity—not somebody else's company. Let me share a funny story that illustrates a CEO really owning delivering against results. This story is from Robin Li, CEO of Baidu, China's biggest search engine company. In a lecture he gave at Stanford University in 2009, Robin recalls that on the day of Baidu's IPO—usually one of an entrepreneur's most exhilarating days in his entire life—he sat at his desk terrified. Why? Listen to how Robin owned delivering results:

> *In 2004, we raised our last round of VC money led by Draper Fisher Jurvetson . . . and Google, one of our great colleagues. Then a year later, in 2005, the company went public. The*

*ideal price was $27 [the stock's initial offer price] and it closed on the first day at $122. It was great for many of the Baidu employees and for all of the Baidu investors. It was a very miserable thing for me because when I decided to take the company public, I was only prepared to deliver financial results that match the price of $27 or maybe a little higher, $30, $40. But I was really shocked to see that the price went to $122 on the first day. So that meant I needed to deliver real results that matched an expectation much, much higher than what I had prepared to do. But in any case, I thought I had no choice. So I put my head down and focused on operations, focused on technology, focused on the user's experience, and I delivered.*

Once we've taken all of this into account, we see that the results against objectives or "black box" results are a *lagging* indicator. And as they say in the mutual fund prospectuses, "past performance is no guarantee of future results." The white-box CEO evaluation criteria— "Does the CEO know what to do?" and "Can the CEO get the company to do it?"—will do a much better job of predicting the future.

## CLOSING THOUGHT

CEO evaluation need not be a byzantine, unarticulated art. All people, including CEOs, will perform better on a test if they know the questions ahead of time.

# CHAPTER 8

# FIRST RULE OF ENTREPRENEURSHIP: THERE ARE NO RULES

"That the that the that that don't kill me

Can only make a me stronger

I need you to hurry up now

'Cause I can't wait much longer

I know I got to be right now

'Cause I can't get much wronger

Man I been waitin' all night now

That's how long I been on ya."

—KANYE WEST, "STRONGER"

When we were in the process of selling Opsware, HP's initial bid came in at $14 per share. BMC countered with $14.05. Then HP countered them with $14.25. John O'Farrell and I planned our strategy for closing the bidding process. We figured that if we executed correctly, the winning bid would come in at $15 per share or higher. Everybody was extremely excited.

Then disaster struck. Or more specifically, our auditor, Ernst & Young, nearly destroyed the deal.

During BMC's diligence process, they discovered that we had accounted for three deals differently than they had. Specifically, each of our three deals contained something that had come to be known in the industry as the "CA clause" in honor of the infamous software company Computer Associates, or CA for short. The CA clause had come about as a result of some of CA's business practices. Apparently CA had tricked their customers by selling them maintenance contracts that gave them rights to free upgrades forever for products named "X." CA would then change the name of product "X" to product "Y" and charge their customers for an upgrade the customers thought they were entitled to for free. It was very clever, and totally dirty. To fight back, savvy customers started requiring all software vendors to include "the CA clause" in their contracts. The clause stated that if you released a new version of your software that contains all of the functionality of the previous version, plus some new features and a new name, then that product (despite the new name) would be covered under the existing contract with no additional fees due.

There were two possible ways to interpret the CA clause. You could either interpret it as it was intended, as a workaround for CA's bad behavior, or you could interpret it as a promise of future functionality. If you interpreted it as the former then you were required to recognize all the revenue up front. If you interpreted it as the latter, then you would recognize the revenue ratably over the course of the contract. In either case, cash payments would be the same.

We understood this ambiguity when we signed the three deals that contained the clause, so we had our E&Y partner, Dave Price, audit the deals and then tell us how we should account for them. Dave correctly understood the intent and recommended that we take the revenue up front in all three deals. BMC's E&Y partner concluded the opposite and they accounted for similar deals ratably. When alerted to the difference, the BMC partner escalated the issue to Ernst & Young's national office.

E&Y's national audit partner called me to report that he now disagreed with his partner's audit and required that we restate revenue guidance in the next forty-eight hours. I couldn't believe what I had just heard. Restating revenue would tank the stock price and destroy the pending sale. The accounting had no material impact on cash flows and our treatment was based on the judgment of Ernst & Young in the first place. If they had accounted for it the other way initially, the stock price would be the same as it is now. It was the restatement that would kill us.

What the hell?

I calmed down and replied carefully.

Ben: "The accounting is meant to reflect the intent of both us and our customers in the contract, correct?"

E&Y: "Correct."

Ben: "So, why don't we call all three customers on the phone and ask them their intent? If it's what Dave Price reflected in our contracts, then we'll leave them as they are. If it's something else, we'll restate revenue."

E&Y: "No. That's not good enough. You'll need to get all three customers to amend their contracts to use new language that we've come up with at E&Y to clear things up."

Ben: "But all three customers are large banks. They have risk departments. They won't just amend their contracts quickly. To make things worse, we are in the middle of a $1.6 billion transaction. You will wreck our deal."

E&Y: "We don't care. That's what you have to do."

Ben: "But we've been a customer for eight years, paid you millions of dollars in fees, and your partner made this judgment to begin with. Why would you destroy our transaction if we and the customers verbally agree with the current interpretation?"

E&Y: "Either amend the contracts or restate your revenue. You have forty-eight hours."

Dave Price looked like he was going to burst into tears.

E&Y's national office did not care about the spirit of the law, only the letter. They refused to do what was right from an accounting or business standpoint. They were determined to do what was optimally convenient for Ernst & Young.

My CFO, Dave Conte, was pale as a ghost. Hundreds of people had worked for eight years to get to this point and it looked like all that work would be flushed down the toilet by the accounting firm that Dave handpicked. He had worked at Ernst & Young for fifteen years before joining Opsware. Normally gregarious and outgoing, he could barely speak. I was furious at everybody but I knew that nothing that I could say would help the problem or make Dave feel any worse than he already felt. I turned to Jordan Breslow, my general counsel, and said, "Do we have to disclose this to the acquirers right away?" Horrifyingly, he said, "Yes."

We told HP and BMC about the discrepancy and that we thought we could resolve the issue by amending the contracts in the next twenty-four hours. Neither party believed us. I don't know if I believed it. How could we possibly get three large banks to amend their contracts in twenty-four hours? Both potential buyers made plans to respond to the news and update their position and possibly their bids.

In the meantime, Dave, Mark Cranney, and I went to work to get the contracts amended. We sat in the finance conference room drawing lines between everybody we knew in the world and tried to figure out how to get to the right people in time to save the deal. I called every board member to see which bank he kept his money in and whether he had any influence or knew somebody with influence. Mark stayed on the phone with the sales reps and the people whom we knew at the accounts. Jordan and Dave came up with ten different ways to word the amendment. We stayed up all night working on the deal and the entire time, Dave looked as though he was having a massive heart attack. Miraculously, by 11 a.m., we got all three contracts amended, and it was in less than twenty-four hours. We would not have to restate revenue.

Not surprisingly, the entire thing spooked BMC, and they withdrew their bid. They did not believe that the issue had been put to bed.

HP wasn't spooked, but they lowered their offer to $13.75 per share due to the "taint" on the deal.

That night the board met in our offices to discuss the new offer from HP and inform them that BMC had dropped out. The board was unanimous in its advice that we should take the $13.75 offer. I disagreed. I said that I would not take a nickel less than the $14.25 originally offered. Bill Campbell looked at me like I was a general who had spent too much time in the field. At that point, I had not slept and didn't know if he was right or wrong. I just knew that I had waited all night to be right and I couldn't get much wronger.

I gathered myself and restated my position: "HP offered $14.25, a price that equals sixteen times trailing twelve months revenue for one reason and one reason only. They offered it because we are the premium company, the gold standard if you will in an important market. That is the entire premise of this deal. The second that we accept a discounted offer or in any other way suggest that we are not the gold standard, this deal falls apart." John O'Farrell nodded in agreement. The board uneasily accepted my position.

I went back to HP and told them the deal would be $14.25 or nothing. After about a two-hour pause, during which time the color never returned to Dave Conte's face, they accepted. We had a deal. A deal for about $100 million less than if our so-called partner had not stabbed us in the back, but a deal nonetheless. I still hate Ernst & Young.


I am telling this story today because just when you think there are things you can count on in business, you quickly find that the sky is purple. When this happens, it usually does no good to keep arguing that the sky is blue. You just have to get on and deal with the fact that it's going to look like Barney for a while.

# SOLVING THE ACCOUNTABILITY VS. CREATIVITY PARADOX

A software engineer identifies a weakness in your current product architecture that will significantly impair its ability to scale down the road. She figures out that she'll have to slip the product schedule three months to fix it. Everybody agrees that three months is an acceptable slip to correct the problem. The schedule actually slips nine months, but she was right about the problem. Do you reward her for her creativity and courage or hold her accountable for the slip?

If you become a prosecuting attorney and hold her to the letter of the law on her commitments, you will almost certainly discourage her and everybody else from taking important risks in the future. If you take this stance consistently, don't be surprised in the future if your people don't have time to solve hard problems because they will be far too busy covering their butts.

On the other hand, if you don't hold her accountable for her commitment, then the people who actually do the work to meet their commitments might feel like idiots. Why did I stay up all night making the deadline if the CEO rewards the person who missed her schedule by six months? If your hardest working, most productive employees feel like chumps and you are looking for the

culprit, look in the mirror. You have failed to hold people accountable for their actions. Welcome to the Accountability vs. Creativity
Paradox.

As we look to solve it, let's start with the most basic assumption.
Do you assume that your employees are by and large creative, intelligent, and motivated? Or do you assume that they are lazy, conniving,
and counting the minutes to quitting time? If you believe the latter,
then you might as well just give up on creativity and innovation in
your organization, because you will not get it. It's better to believe the
former and assume that people have good intentions unless they prove
otherwise. Still, you must hold people accountable to avoid the chump
factor. How do you think about that?

Let's look at accountability across the following dimensions: promises, results, and effort.

## ACCOUNTABILITY FOR EFFORT

This is the easy one. To be a world-class company, you need world-
class effort. If somebody isn't giving it to you, they must be checked.

## ACCOUNTABILITY FOR PROMISES

A lot of good-running organizations have statements like "make a
commitment, keep a commitment." It's true that if you sign up for
something and you don't do it, you let everyone in the organization
down. This type of letdown can be contagious. Holding people accountable for their promises is a critical factor in getting things done.
This changes as the degree of difficulty in fulfilling the promise increases. Promising to complete a piece of marketing collateral or send
an email is different from promising to meet an engineering schedule that involves solving some fundamentally hard computer science

problem. You must hold people accountable for the former; the latter is more complicated and relates to results.

## ACCOUNTABILITY FOR RESULTS

This is where things get complicated. If someone fails to deliver the result she promised, as in the opening story, must you hold her accountable? Should you hold her accountable? The answer is that it depends. It depends upon:

- **Seniority of the employee** You should expect experienced people to be able to forecast their results more accurately than junior people.

- **Degree of difficulty** Some things are just plain hard. Making your sales number when your product is inferior to the competition and a recession hits midquarter is hard. Building a platform that automatically and efficiently takes serial programs and parallelizes them, so that they can scale out, is hard. It's hard to make a good prediction and hard to meet that prediction. When deciding the consequence of missing a result, you must take into account the degree of difficulty.

- **Amount of stupid risk** While you don't want to punish people for taking good risks, not all risks are good. While there is no reward without risk, there is certainly risk with little or no chance of corresponding reward. Drinking a bottle of Jack Daniel's then getting behind the wheel of a car is plenty risky, but there's not much reward if you succeed. If someone missed a result, did she take obviously stupid risks that she just neglected to consider, or were they excellent risks that just did not pan out?

## REVISITING THE OPENING PROBLEM

So looking back at the opening problem, here are some things to consider:

1. *How senior is she?* If she's your chief architect, you'll need her to get better at scoping her work or she's going to trash the organization. If she is more junior, this should be more a teaching moment than a scolding moment.

2. *How hard was it?* If it was a miracle that you ever made that piece of crap scale, then you shouldn't yell at her. In fact, you should thank her. If it was a relatively trivial project that just took too long, then you need to address that.

3. *Was the original risk the right one to take?* Would the product really have run out of scale in the short-to-medium term? If the answer is yes, then whether it took three months or nine months, it was the right risk to take and if faced with the same situation again, you probably should not change any of your actions. You shouldn't be wringing your hands about that.

## FINAL POINT

In the technology business, you rarely know everything up front. The difference between being mediocre and magical is often the difference between letting people take creative risk and holding them too tightly accountable. Accountability is important, but it's not the only thing that's important.

# THE FREAKY FRIDAY
# MANAGEMENT TECHNIQUE

Many years ago, I encountered a particularly tricky management situation. Two excellent teams in the company, Customer Support and Sales Engineering, went to war with each other. The sales engineers escalated a series of blistering complaints arguing that the Customer Support team did not respond with urgency, refused to fix issues in the product, and generally inhibited sales and customer satisfaction. Meanwhile, the Customer Support group claimed that the sales engineers submitted bugs without qualification, did not listen to valid suggested fixes, and were alarmists who assigned every issue the top priority. Beyond the actual complaints, the teams genuinely did not like each other. To make matters worse, these groups had to work together constantly in order for the company to function. Both teams boasted superb personnel and outstanding managers, so there was nobody to fire or demote. I could not figure out what to do.

Around this time, I miraculously happened to watch the motion picture classic *Freaky Friday*, starring the underrated Barbara Harris and the incomparable Jodie Foster. (There is also a high-quality remake starring Jamie Lee Curtis and the troubled but talented Lindsay Lohan.) In the film, mother and daughter grow completely frustrated with each other's lack of understanding and wish that they could switch places and, through the magic of film, they do.

Through the course of the movie, by being inside each other's bodies, both characters develop an understanding of the challenges that the other faces. As a result, the two become great friends when they switch back. After watching both the original and the remake, I knew that I had found the answer: I would employ a *Freaky Friday* management technique.

The very next day I informed the head of Sales Engineering and the head of Customer Support that they would be switching jobs. I explained that, like Jodie Foster and Barbara Harris, they would keep their minds, but get new bodies. Permanently. Their initial reactions were not unlike the remake where Lindsay Lohan and Jamie Lee Curtis both scream in horror.

However, after just one week walking in the other's moccasins, both executives quickly diagnosed the core issues causing the conflict. They then swiftly acted to implement a simple set of processes that cleared up the combat and got the teams working harmoniously. From that day to the day we sold the company, the Sales Engineering and Customer Support organizations worked better together than any other major groups in the company—all thanks to *Freaky Friday*, perhaps the most insightful management training film ever made.

# STAYING GREAT

As CEO, you know that you cannot build a world-class company unless you maintain a world-class team. But how do you know if an executive is world-class? Beyond that, if she was world-class when you hired her, will she stay world-class? If she doesn't, will she become world-class again?

These are complex questions and are made more complex by the courting process. Every CEO sets out to hire the very best person in the world and then recruits aggressively to get him. If he says yes, she inevitably thinks she's hit the jackpot. If I had a tattoo for every time I heard a CEO claim that she'd just hired "the best VP in the industry," I'd be Lil Wayne.

So we begin with a strong bias that whoever we hired must be world-class even before performing one day of work. To make matters worse, executives who start off world-class often deteriorate over time. If you are a sports fan, you know that world-class athletes don't stay world-class for long. One day you are Terrell Owens and the next day you are Terrell Owens. While executives don't age nearly as fast as athletes do, companies, markets, and technologies change a thousand times faster than the game of football. As a result, the executive who is spectacular in this year's hundred-person startup may be washed-up in next year's version when the company employs four hundred people and has $100 million in revenue.

## THE STANDARD

The first thing to understand is that just because somebody interviewed well and reference-checked great, that does not mean she will perform superbly in your company. There are two kinds of cultures in this world: cultures where what you do matters and cultures where all that matters is who you are. You can be the former or you can suck.

You must hold your people to a high standard, but what is that standard? I discussed this in the section "Old People." In addition, keep the following in mind:

- *You did not know everything when you hired her.* While it feels awkward, it is perfectly reasonable to change and raise your standards as you learn more about what's needed and what's competitive in your industry.

- *You must get leverage.* Early on, it's natural to spend a great deal of time integrating and orienting an executive. However, if you find yourself as busy as you were with that function before you hired or promoted the executive, then she is below standard.

- *As CEO, you can do very little employee development.* One of the most depressing lessons of my career when I became CEO was that I could not develop the people who reported to me. The demands of the job made it such that the people who reported to me had to be 99 percent ready to perform. Unlike when I ran a function or was a general manager, there was no time to develop raw talent. That can and must be done elsewhere in the company, but not at the executive level. If someone needs lots of training, she is below standard.

It is possible to take the standard setting too far. As I discussed in the section "The Scale Anticipation Fallacy," it's neither necessary nor a good idea to evaluate an executive based on what her job will be two years from now. You can cross that bridge when you come to it. Evaluate her on how she performs right here and right now.

## ON EXPECTATIONS AND LOYALTY

If you have a great and loyal executive, how do you communicate all this? How do you tell her that despite the massive effort and great job she is doing today, you might fire her next year if she doesn't keep up with the changes in the business?

When I used to review executives, I would tell them, "You are doing a great job at your current job, but the plan says that we will have twice as many employees next year as we have right now. Therefore, you will have a new and very different job and I will have to reevaluate you on the basis of that job. If it makes you feel better, that rule goes for everyone on the team, including me."

In providing this kind of direction, it's important to point out to the executive that when the company doubles in size, she has a new job. This means that doing things that made her successful in her old job will not necessarily translate to success in the new job. In fact, the number-one way that executives fail is by continuing to do their old job rather than moving on to their new job.

But, what about being loyal to the team that got you here? If your current executive team helped you grow your company tenfold, how can you dismiss them when they fall behind in running the behemoth they created? The answer is that your loyalty must go to your employees—the people who report to your executives. Your engineers, marketing people, salespeople, and finance and HR people who are doing the work. You owe them a world-class management team. That's the priority.

# SHOULD YOU SELL
# YOUR COMPANY?

One of the most difficult decisions that a CEO ever makes is whether to sell her company. Logically, determining whether selling a company will be better in the long term than continuing to run it stand-alone involves a huge number of factors, most of which are speculative or unknown. And if you are the founder, the logical part is the easy part.

The task would be far simpler if there were no emotion involved. But selling your company is always emotional and deeply personal.

## TYPES OF ACQUISITIONS

For the purpose of this discussion, it is useful to think about technology acquisitions in three categories:

1. **Talent and/or technology,** when a company is acquired purely for its technology and/or its people. These kinds of deals typically range between $5 million and $50 million.

2. **Product,** when a company is acquired for its product, but not its business. The acquirer plans to sell the product roughly as it is, but will do so primarily with its own sales

and marketing capability. These kinds of deals typically range between $25 million and $250 million.

3. **Business,** when a company is acquired for its actual business (revenue and earnings). The acquirer values the entire operation (product, sales, and marketing), not just the people, technology, or products. These deals are typically valued (at least in part) by their financial metrics and can be extremely large (such as Microsoft's $30 billion–plus offer for Yahoo).

My take on the subject is most applicable to *business* acquisitions, with some relevance to *product* acquisitions, and will be fairly useless if you are selling people and/or technology.

## THE LOGICAL

When analyzing whether you should sell your company, a good basic rule of thumb is if (a) you are very early on in a very large market *and* (b) you have a good chance of being number one in that market, then you should remain stand-alone. The reason is that nobody will be able to afford to pay what you are worth, because nobody can give you that much forward credit. For an easy-to-understand example, consider Google. When they were very early, they reportedly received multiple acquisition offers for more than $1 billion. These were considered very rich offers at the time and they amounted to a gigantic multiple. However, given the size of the ultimate market, it did not make sense for Google to sell. In fact, it didn't make sense for Google to sell to any suitor at any price that the buyer could have paid. Why? Because the market that Google was pursuing was actually bigger than the markets that all of the potential buyers owned and Google had built a nearly invincible product lead that enabled them to be number one.

Contrast this situation with Pointcast. Pointcast was one of the first Internet applications to catch fire. They were the buzz of Silicon

Valley and the technology industry in general. They received billion-dollar acquisition offers that they passed on. Then, due to flaws in their product architecture, their customers started to turn off their application. Overnight, their market collapsed and never returned. They were ultimately sold for a relatively tiny amount.

So, the judgment that you have to make is (a) is this market really much bigger (more than an order of magnitude) than has been exploited to date? and (b) are we going to be number one? If the answer to either (a) or (b) is no, then you should consider selling. If the answers to both are yes, then selling would mean selling yourself and your employees short.

Unfortunately, these questions are not as simple to answer as I've made them out to be. In order to get the answer right, you also have to answer the question "What is the market, really, and who are the competitors going to be?" Was Google in the search market or the portal market? In retrospect, they were in the search market, but most people thought they were in the portal market at the time. Yahoo was a tough competitor in the portal market, but not so much in the search market. If Google had really been in the portal market, then selling might have been a good idea. Pointcast thought that their market was much larger than it turned out to be. Interestingly, Pointcast's own product execution (or lack thereof) caused their market to shrink.

Let's look at the case of Opsware. Why did I sell Opsware? Another good question is why didn't I sell Opsware until I did?

At Opsware, we started in the server automation market. When we received our first inquiries and offers for the server automation company, we had fewer than fifty customers. I believed that there were at least ten thousand target customers and that we had a decent shot at being number one. In addition, although I knew the market would be redefined, I thought that we could expand to networks and storage (data center automation) faster than the competition and win that market as well. Therefore, assuming 30 percent market share, somebody would have had to pay sixty times what we were worth in forward credit to buy out our potential. You won't be surprised to find that nobody was willing to pay that.

Once we grew to several hundred customers and expanded into data center automation, we were still number one and were more valuable stand-alone than any of the prior acquisition offers. At that point both Opsware and our main competitor, BladeLogic, had developed into full-fledged companies (worldwide sales forces, built-out professional services, etc.). This was significant, because it meant that a large company could buy one of us and potentially execute successfully (big enterprise companies can't generally succeed with small acquisitions, because too much of the important intellectual property is the sales methodology, and big companies can't build that).

At this point, it became clear that BMC was going to buy either Opsware or BladeLogic. As a result, the calculus, or whether Opsware was going to be number one in the market, needed to be redefined as follows:

1. We had to be number one in the systems and network management market rather than the data center automation market, because like the word processor market, the data center automation market was going to be subsumed by a larger market that contained it.

2. In order to be number one, we had to beat BMC and Blade-Logic together, which was a significantly more difficult opponent than either company stand-alone.

Finally, the market itself was transforming due to an underlying technological shift: virtualization. Virtualization meant that the entire market needed to be retooled, so we were embarking on a new R&D race to build the best management for virtualized environments. This meant deferring earnings for a very long time.

Based on all these factors, it made sense for us to at least consider the possibility of acquisition and run a short process to understand the interest in the M&A market.

Through that process, eleven companies made acquisition offers of some form. This told me that we were at a local maxima in terms of the market price for Opsware. In other words, the set of potential buyers was convinced that the market was very important, and there was no extra premium that we could hope to achieve through better awareness. In the end, based on a lot of analysis and soul-searching, I determined that the current local maxima was higher than we could expect to achieve in the next three to five years and I sold the company to Hewlett-Packard for $1.65 billion. I think and hope that was the right decision.


## THE EMOTIONAL

The funny thing about the emotional part of the decision is that it's so schizophrenic.

How can you ever sell your company after you've personally re-cruited every employee and sold them on your spectacular vision of a thriving, stand-alone business? How can you ever sell out your dream?

How can you walk away from total financial independence for yourself and every member of your close and distant family? Aren't you in business to make money? How much money does one person need?

How can you reconcile *Dr. Stay-the-Course* and *Mr. Sell-the-Thing*? Clearly they are irreconcilable, but the key is to mute them both.

A few keys on muting the emotions:

- *Get paid (a salary).* Most venture capitalists like entre-preneurs that are "all in," meaning the entrepreneur has everything invested in the company and will have very little to show for her efforts if it does not succeed. As part of this, they prefer the founding CEO to have a very low salary. In general, this is a good idea, because the temptation to walk away when things go poorly is intense and total financial commitment helps him to keep his other commitments. However, once the company starts to become a company rather than an idea it makes sense to pay the CEO at market. More specifically, once the company has a business (as defined above) and becomes an attractive acquisition target, it makes sense to pay the CEO, so that the decision to keep or sell the company isn't a direct response to the CEO's personal financial situation, as in "I don't think that we should sell the company, but I live in an eight-hundred-fifty-square-foot apartment with my husband and two kids and it's that or divorce."

■ *Be clear with the company.* One question that every startup CEO gets from her employees is "Are you selling the company?" This is an incredibly difficult question. If she says nothing, the employee will likely interpret this to mean the company is for sale. If she says "at the right price," the employee will wonder what that price is and may even ask. If the company ever reaches that price, the employee will assume the company will be sold. If she dodges the question with the standard "the company is not for sale," the employee may feel betrayed if the company is ever sold. More important, the CEO may feel like she is betraying the employee and that feeling will influence her decision-making process. One way to avoid these traps is to describe the analysis in the prior section: If the company achieves product-market fit in a very large market and has an excellent chance to be number one, then the company will likely remain independent. If not, it will likely be sold. This is one good method to describe the interests of the investors in a way that's not at odds with the interests of the employees, and it is true.

## FINAL THOUGHT

When faced with the decision of whether to sell your company, there is no easy answer. However, preparing yourself intellectually and emotionally will help.

# CHAPTER 9

# THE END OF THE BEGINNING

"We walk the same path, but got on different shoes
Live in the same building, but we got different views."
−DRAKE, "RIGHT ABOVE IT"

After selling Opsware, I spent a year at HP running the bulk of their software business. And then I tried to figure out what to do next. Should I start another company? Should I be CEO of someone else's company? Should I retire? Should I do something completely different?

The more I thought about my future, the more I thought about my past. What would have happened if I'd never met Bill Campbell? How would I have possibly worked my way through all the challenges I'd faced? Why was entrepreneurship such a black art? Did everybody have the same problems I'd had? If they did, why didn't anybody write anything down? Why did so few startup advisers and venture capitalists have any experience starting companies?

As these thoughts rolled around in my head, I sent Marc Andreessen an instant message: "We ought to start a venture capital firm. Our motto for general partners would be 'some experience required' as in some experience in founding and running companies is required to advise people who are founding and running companies." To my surprise, he replied, "I was thinking the same thing."

## SOME EXPERIENCE NECESSARY

Further contemplation took me back to one of my first serious encounters with venture capital.

Back in 1999, after raising our first round of funding for Loudcloud, my cofounders and I went to visit our new venture capital firm and meet their full team. As founding CEO, I remember being excited to meet our financial backers and to talk about how we could partner to build a great company. The conversation took a sharp downhill turn when one of the senior partners, David Beirne, asked me, in front of my cofounders, "When are you going to get a real CEO?"

The comment knocked the wind out of me. Our largest investor had basically called me a fake CEO in front of my team. I asked, "What do you mean?"—hoping he would revise his statement and enable me to save face. Instead he pressed on: "Someone who has designed a large organization, someone who knows great senior executives and brings prebuilt customer relationships, someone who knows what they are doing."

I could hardly breathe. It was bad enough that he had undermined my standing as CEO, but to make matters worse, I knew that at some level he was right. I didn't have those skills. I had never *done* those things. And I did not know those people. I was the founding CEO, not a professional CEO. I could almost hear the clock ticking in the background as my time running the company quickly ran out. Could I learn the job and build my network fast enough or would I lose the company? That question tortured me for months.

In the years that followed, I remained CEO, for better or worse. I worked incredibly hard to become the kind of CEO that everyone expected. Thanks to a lot of effort and help from friends and mentors, especially Bill Campbell, the company survived and became successful and valuable.

Not a day went by, however, when I didn't think about that interaction with David Beirne. I always wondered how long I had to grow up and how I could find help to build my skills and make the necessary connections along the way.

Marc and I discussed this paradox often. We wondered aloud why as founders we had to prove to our investors beyond a shadow of a doubt that we could run the company, rather than our investors assuming that we would run the company we'd created. This conversation ultimately became the inspiration for Andreessen Horowitz.

To get started, we studied the venture capital industry and we came across a potential problem with our approach. Historically, all the returns in venture capital had been concentrated in a tiny number of firms and consistently by a small number of the same firms. Of the more than eight hundred venture capital firms of the day, only about six had delivered great returns for their investors. As we dug deeper, we uncovered an excellent reason for this: The best entrepreneurs will only work with the best venture capital firms. Since venture capital firms were notoriously secretive about their methods and beliefs— most firms did almost no PR and stated very little about what they did—the firms competed on their investing track records. Therefore, the firms with the best track records continued to have the best track records, thus making it nearly impossible for a new firm, with no track record, to crack into the top tier.

We needed some way to break through to become the firm that great entrepreneurs wanted to work with. But how?

We needed to change the rules by which entrepreneurs evaluated VCs. We thought there was an opening to do this, because times had changed. When Marc and I first became entrepreneurs back in the mid-1990s, we did not know many other entrepreneurs. We just did what we did, without really seeing ourselves as part of a larger "movement" or a community. We were entrepreneurs at the beginning of the Internet and before Facebook, Twitter, and the other social networking platforms were built. We did not talk to other entrepreneurs, because there was no entrepreneurial community. We were completely heads down on the business. All that has changed in the last ten years.

Entrepreneurs are now socializing, friending each other, meeting up, and hanging out. There is a real community. Once we realized this, we figured that if we had a better offering, word-of-mouth marketing would work now where it hadn't before.

We needed to be better, but we also needed to be different. As we thought about what would make us both better and different, two core ideas greatly influenced our thinking: First, technical founders are the best people to run technology companies. All of the long-lasting technology companies that we admired—Hewlett-Packard, Intel, Amazon, Apple, Google, Facebook—had been run by their founders. More specifically, the innovator was running the company. Second, it was incredibly difficult for technical founders to learn to become CEOs while building their companies. I was a testament to that. But, most venture capital firms were better designed to replace the founder than to help the founder grow and succeed.

Marc and I thought that if we created a firm specifically designed to help technical founders run their own companies, we could develop a reputation and a brand that might vault us into the top tier of venture capital firms despite having no track record. We identified two key deficits that a founder CEO had when compared with a professional CEO:

1. **The CEO skill set** Managing executives, organizational design, running sales organizations and the like were all important skills that technical founders lacked.

2. **The CEO network** Professional CEOs knew lots of executives, potential customers and partners, people in the press, investors, and other important business connections. Technical founders, on the other hand, knew some good engineers and how to program.

Next, we asked, "How might a venture capital firm help founder CEOs close those gaps?"

Addressing the skill set issue proved to be difficult because, sadly, the only way to learn how to be a CEO is to be a CEO. Sure, we might try to teach some skills, but learning to be a CEO through classroom training would be like learning to be an NFL quarterback through classroom training. Even if Peyton Manning and Tom Brady were your instructors, in the absence of hands-on experience, you'd get killed the moment you took the field.

We decided that while we would not be able to give a founder CEO all the skills she needed, we would be able to provide the kind of mentorship that would accelerate the learning process. As a result, we decided that all of our general partners would need to be effective mentors for a founder striving to be a CEO. (Of course, not all founders want to be CEO. For some companies, the right thing is to bring in a professional CEO. For those companies, we would focus on helping the founders identify the right CEO, and then helping the CEO successfully integrate into the company and partner with the founders to retain their unique strengths.) This is why so many of the general partners we choose are former founders or CEOs or both, and they are all highly focused on helping founders become outstanding CEOs. The idea seemed so simple and obvious that it had to work.

Next, we decided to systematize and professionalize the network. For this we drew both the inspiration and the formula from my friend and Opsware board member Michael Ovitz. Thirty-four years earlier, Michael had founded Creative Artists Agency (CAA), the powerhouse of Hollywood talent agencies. When Michael started CAA, it was not an obvious idea. The talent agency business had existed since vaudeville and had changed very little in the ensuing seventy-five years. Michael was a rising star at the William Morris Agency, the most important agency in the industry at the time. Quitting that job to pursue what must have looked like a windmill tilt made no sense to anybody. But Michael had a clear vision: If he could build a firm so good that it attracted all the top talent in the world, then he would shift the economics of the industry from the corporations to the talent, where he felt that it belonged.

The firms of the day were essentially collections of loosely affiliated talent agents. Agents worked under the same umbrella, but acted largely alone, each agent tapping into her own network on behalf of her own clients. For example, Agent A might introduce Dustin Hoffman to the head of Warner Bros., but both the relationship with Dustin Hoffman and the relationship with Warner Bros. were controlled entirely by the agent; other William Morris agents and clients didn't automatically get access to either. This traditional model sounded a lot like the traditional venture capital business, where VCs worked in the same firm but managed their own networks and their own portfolios.

Ovitz's breakthrough idea was to build an integrated network that would allow any of the firm's agents to connect their clients to a firm-wide grid of new opportunities. As a result, the firm would be a hundred times more powerful than any one agent at any other agency. To implement the idea, Ovitz and his founding partners agreed to defer their salaries for several years and invest their commissions into building what Ovitz referred to as "The Franchise." The Franchise consisted of specialists running networks and portfolios in each relevant area: book publishing, international, music, and more. His theory worked, and within fifteen years, CAA represented 90 percent of the top talent in Hollywood and had rewritten the rules—giving talent more say in deals and a bigger piece of the financial pie.

We decided to copy CAA's operating model nearly exactly—in fact, Andreessen Horowitz employees have the same titles as the original CAA employees: partner. Michael thought it was a great idea, but he was the only one. Everyone else offered some variation of the following: "This is Silicon Valley, not Hollywood. You guys don't understand the business." Still, with Michael's endorsement and enthusiastic support, we pushed forward with the idea. As we applied it to venture capital, we decided to build the following networks:

- **Large companies** Every new company needs to either sell something to or partner with a larger company.

- **Executives** If you succeed, at some point you need to hire executives.

- **Engineers** In the technology business, you can never know enough great engineers.

- **Press and analysts** We have a saying around the firm: Show it, sell it; hide it, keep it.

- **Investors and acquirers** Being venture capitalists, providing access to money was obvious.

Once we designed the firm, we needed to help entrepreneurs understand how we were different. This seemed tricky, because no major venture capital firm did any marketing of any kind. We figured there must be a good explanation for this, but struggled to find one. Finally, Marc discovered that the original venture capital firms in the late 1940s and early '50s were modeled after the original investment banks such as J.P. Morgan and Rothschild. Those banks also did not do PR for a very specific reason: The banks funded wars—and sometimes both sides of the same war—so publicity was not a good idea. This insight, combined with our general instinct to counterprogram whatever the big guys were doing, led us to launch Andreessen Horowitz with great fanfare. When deciding on the name, the biggest problem we faced was that, as a firm, we were nobodies. No track record, no portfolio companies, no nothing. But people knew us and they especially knew Marc. So I said, "Rather than trying to create a totally new brand from scratch, why not just use your brand?" Marc thought that made sense, but nobody would ever be able to spell "Andreessen Horowitz" when typing in the URL. Thinking back to old-time computer programming in the days before programming languages supported internationalization, we used to have to "internationalize" our code. We called this internationalization process "I18N" for short (localization was L10N), which meant *I* followed by eighteen letters followed by *N*. We decided that the firm's nickname would be "a16z," as in *a* followed by sixteen letters followed by *z*.

We hired the Outcast marketing agency, headed up by its formidable founder, Margit Wennmachers, to generate media interest. We needed people to know what we were about as we had decided to defy the conventional venture capital theory of no PR. The daughter of a German pig farmer, Margit was the furthest thing from a swine wrangler imaginable. Smart and sophisticated, she was the Babe Ruth of PR. She worked her contacts, landing a cover story in *Fortune* in 2009 that featured Marc posing as Uncle Sam. Andreessen Horowitz was an overnight sensation, and yet Marc and I were still the only two people in the firm.

After eight years of running Loudcloud and Opsware, I had learned so many hard lessons that building the team was easy. I understood the importance of hiring for strength rather than for lack of weakness, and I understood the meaning of "fit." There are lots of smart people in the world, but smart is not good enough. I needed people who were great where I needed greatness. I needed people who really wanted to do the jobs they were hired for. And I needed people who believed in the mission—to make Silicon Valley a better place to build a company.

The first person we hired was Scott Kupor, who had been the director of finance from Opsware. Scott worked for me for nearly the entire eight years, and I'm not sure that he enjoyed any of it, but he performed phenomenally nonetheless. He ran customer support, planning, and technical field operations during those years, but none of the jobs were what he wanted to do. Scott loved three tasks: running things, strategy, and deals. If he could do those things, he'd almost never sleep. But at Opsware, he'd only gotten to do two of the three. Not getting to work on transactions was torture for Scott. He was like a caged animal. And I'd kept him in that cage for eight long years. So, when we designed the firm, the first thing that came to my mind was "I finally found the perfect job for Kupor." Scott became the firm's chief operating officer.

We then filled out the rest of the team. We hired Mark Cranney, head of sales at Opsware, to run the large-company network; Shannon Callahan, former head of recruiting and HR, to run the engineering network; Margit Wennmachers, the Sultan of Swat, to run the marketing network; Jeff Stump, the best executive recruiter we knew, to run the executive network; and Frank Chen, my former head of product management, to run a centralized research group.

Our theory about what a venture capital firm should offer turned out to resonate with the best entrepreneurs in the world. In four very short years, we have gone from nothing to being one of the most respected venture capital firms in the world.

## FINAL LESSON

"I know you think my life is good cause my diamond piece
But my life been good since I started finding peace."
—NAS, "LOCO-MOTIVE"

I often joke that I am considered to be a much better CEO now than I was when I was actually CEO. These days people sometimes refer to me as a management guru, but when I managed Opsware most people referred to me as, well, less than that. As Felicia is fond of saying, "They called you everything but a child of God."

What happened? Did I change or did perception change?

There is no question that I learned a great deal over the years and I am pretty embarrassed about how I conducted myself in the early days, but by the end I became pretty good at running the company. There is plenty of evidence supporting this view. I completely changed our business midstream—even while it was a publicly traded company—and still managed to grow its value from $29 million to $1.65 billion in five years. A large percentage of the employees from Opsware either work for me at Andreessen Horowitz or in one of our portfolio companies, so they must have liked something about working together. The acquisition by HP was the largest outcome in the sector, so we won our market.

Still, during the years that I was good at running Opsware—from 2003 to 2007—you would be hard-pressed to find a single article or blog post or message board comment that said anything nice about me. During that time, the press declared the company dead and shareholders called for my resignation. No, I was not considered to be very good at all.

In retrospect, people's perceptions changed because of the sale to HP and the things that I've since written. Once I stopped being CEO, I was granted a freedom that I did not have before. As a venture capitalist, I have had the freedom to say what I want and what I really think without worrying what everybody else thinks. As a CEO, there is no such luxury. As CEO, I had to worry about what everybody else thought. In particular, I could not show weakness in public. It would not have been fair to the employees, the executives, or the public company shareholders. Unrelenting confidence was necessary.

When we started Andreessen Horowitz, I could let all that go. Sure, we still have employees, but we do not have public shareholders who live and die on every piece of press. More important, at Andreessen Horowitz I am not really CEO. We invest in companies that have CEOs. The burden of unrelenting confidence lies with them. I can now share my weaknesses, my fears, and my shortcomings. I can say what I want without worrying about offending the wrong people in the power structure. And it's those fears and controversial opinions that hold the clues to dealing with hard things. Hard things are hard because there are no easy answers or recipes. They are hard because your emotions are at odds with your logic. They are hard because you don't know the answer and you cannot ask for help without showing weakness.

When I first became a CEO, I genuinely thought that I was the only one struggling. Whenever I spoke to other CEOs, they all seemed like they had everything under control. Their businesses were always going "fantastic" and their experience was inevitably "amazing." I thought that maybe growing up in Berkeley with Communist grandparents might not have been the best background for running a company. But as I watched my peers' fantastic, amazing businesses go bankrupt and sell for cheap, I realized that I was probably not the only one struggling.

As I got further into it, I realized that embracing the unusual parts of my background would be the key to making it through. It would be those things that would give me unique perspectives and approaches to the business. The things that I would bring to the table that nobody else had. It was my borrowing Chico Mendoza's shocking yet poetic style to motivate and focus the team. It was my understanding of the people underneath the persona and skin color that enabled me to put Jason Rosenthal together with Anthony Wright to save the company. It was even my bringing in to the most capitalistic pursuit imaginable what Karl Marx got right. On my grandfather's tombstone, you will find his favorite Marx quote: "Life is struggle." I believe that within that quote lies the most important lesson in entrepreneurship: Embrace the struggle.

When I work with entrepreneurs today, this is the main thing that I try to convey. Embrace your weirdness, your background, your instinct. If the keys are not in there, they do not exist. I can relate to what they're going through, but I cannot tell them what to do. I can only help them find it in themselves. And sometimes they can find peace where I could not.

Of course, even with all the advice and hindsight in the world, hard things will continue to be hard things. So, in closing, I just say peace to all those engaged in the struggle to fulfill their dreams.

# QUESTIONS FOR HEAD
# OF ENTERPRISE SALES FORCE

**Is she smart enough?**

- Can she effectively pitch you on her current company?

- How articulate is she on the company and market opportunity that you are presenting to her now?

- Will she be able to contribute to the strategic direction of your company in a meaningful way?

**Does she know how to hire salespeople?**

- What is her profile?

- Ask her to describe a recent bad hire.

- How does she find top talent?

- What percentage of her time is spent recruiting?

- How does she test for the characteristics she wants with her interview process?

- How many of her current people want to sign up? Can you reference them and validate that?

- Could you pass her sales interview test? Should you be able to pass?

- Does she know how to hire sales managers?

- Can she define the job?

- Can she test for the skills?

**Is she systematic and comprehensive on how she thinks about the sales process?**

- Does she understand the business and the technical sales processes?

- Does she understand benchmarking, lockout documents, proof of concepts, demos?

- Does she know how to train people to become competent in the process?

- Can she enforce the process?

- What is her expectation of her team's use of the CRM tools?

- Did she run the process at her last company or did she write the process?

There is a big difference between people who can write a game plan and people who can follow a game plan.

**How good is her sales training program?**

- How much process training versus product training? Can she describe it in detail?

- Does she have materials?

- How effective is her sales rep evaluation model?

- Can she get beyond basic performance?

- Can she describe the difference between a transactional rep and an enterprise rep in a way that teaches you something?

**Does she understand the ins and outs of setting up a comp plan?**
- Accelerators, spiffs, etc.

**Does she know how to do big deals?**

- Has she made existing deals much larger? Will her people be able to describe that? Has she accelerated the close of a large deal?

- Does she have customers who will reference this?

- Does she understand marketing?

- Can she articulate the differences between brand marketing, lead generation, and sales force enablement without prompting?

**Does she understand channels?**

- Does she really understand channel conflict and incentives?

- Is she intense enough?

- Will the rep in Wisconsin wake up at 5 a.m. and hit the phones or will they wake up at noon and have lunch?

**Can she run international?**

**Is she totally plugged into the industry?**

## How quickly can she diagnose?

- Does she know your competition?

- Does she know what deals you are in right now?

- Has she mapped your organization?

# OPERATIONAL EXCELLENCE QUESTIONS

### Managing Direct Reports

- What do you look for in the people working for you?

- How do you figure that out in the interview process?

- How do you train them for success?

- What is your process for evaluating them?

### Decision-Making

- What methods do you use to get the information that you need in order to make decisions?

- How do you make decisions (what is the process)?

- How do you run your staff meeting? What is the agenda?

- How do you manage actions and promises?

- How do you systematically get your knowledge?

  - □ Of the organization

  - □ Of the customers

  - □ Of the market

**Core management processes–please describe how you've designed these and why.**

- Interview

- Performance management

- Employee integration

- Strategic planning

**Metric Design**

- Describe the key leading and lagging indicators for your organization.

- Are they appropriately paired? For example, do you value time, but not quality?

- Are there potentially negative side effects?

- What was the process that you used to design them?

**Organizational Design**

- Describe your current organizational design.

- What are the strengths and weaknesses?

- Why?

- Why did you opt for those strengths and weaknesses (why were the strengths more important)?

- What are the conflicts? How do they get resolved?

## Confrontation

- If your best executive asks you for more territory, how do you handle it?

- Describe your process for both promotion and firing.

- How do you deal with chronic bad behavior from a top performer?

## Less Tangible

- Does she think systematically or one-off?

- Would I want to work for her?

- Is she totally honest or is she bullshitty?

- Does she ask me spontaneous incisive questions or only pre-prepared ones?

- Can she handle diverse communication styles?

- Is she incredibly articulate?

- Has she done her homework on the company?

# ACKNOWLEDGMENTS

First and most important, I thank my beautiful wife of twenty-five years, Felicia Horowitz. It is a little odd thanking her, because she has been so central to the story that she is more properly the coauthor. She has been my number-one supporter and her belief in me and in this book has meant everything. There would be no book without her, and there is no me without her. She is my partner in life and the love of my life, and I owe her everything that I have and everything that I am. I do not have the words to express the magnitude of gratitude that I feel. Felicia, I love you and I thank you.

I am extremely grateful to the countless people who helped me through all the difficult times and to the people who helped me articulate what all that was like. I hope this book pays some of that forward.

Next my mother, Elissa Horowitz, who always encouraged me to pursue anything that I wanted to do—from playing football to writing this book. She believed in me when nobody else did and understood me like nobody else ever could. Thanks, Mom!

I also thank my father, David, who convinced me that writing this book was a good idea and then put in long hours helping me edit it.

None of this would have been possible without my longtime business partner Marc Andreessen seeing things in me that nobody else did. Beyond that, it's been amazing to work with him for the past eighteen years. He's been a great inspiration to me in everything that I do. He was the primary editor of the first dozen blog posts that I wrote and a very helpful editor of this book. It's a great privilege for me to work with someone of his caliber every day.

I thank my friend Bill Campbell for teaching me so many things about how to survive the hard times. So few people went through what he went through and almost nobody is willing to talk about it. Bill, thank you for your honesty and courage.

Michael Ovitz helped me rewrite the ending of the book and make it ten times better. Before that, he did everything imaginable to support me in my impossible quest—up to and including buying Opsware stock when nobody else would. He is a true friend.

To every employee who ever worked at Loudcloud or Opsware, I thank you from the bottom of my heart. I still cannot believe that you believed in me as much as I believed in you. On that team, very special thanks to Jason Rosenthal, Mark Cranney, Sharmila Mulligan, Dave Conte, John O'Farrell, Jordan Breslow, Scott Kupor, Ted Crossman, and Anthony Wright for being part of this book. Hopefully, I didn't get anything too wrong. Thank you, Eric Vishria, Eric Thomas, Ken Tinsley, and Peter Thorp, for helping me remember what happened. Thanks also to Ray Soursa, Phil Liu, and Paul Ingram for saving the company. Darwin forever! Thanks so much, Shannon Callahan. I still cannot believe that I laid you off. Thanks to Dave Jagoda for not letting me forget what matters.

I thank Tim Howes, my Loudcloud/Opsware cofounder and confidant. I do not know if we made all the right decisions, but I do know that our conversations kept me sane. Thank you for being there from start to finish.

Without Carlye Adler, my editor and coach, I am not sure that I would have even started this book, let alone finished it. Nobody was more jazzed when I wrote something good or sadder when I wrote something boring. Thank you, Carlye, for making this book so much better than it should have been.

Special thanks to Hollis Heimbouch for tracking me down on Facebook and getting me to write the book. I could not have asked for a better publisher. A thank-you to the entire team at HarperCollins.

Binky Urban is the top literary agent in the world, and I am so lucky to have had the chance to be her client. It is a great joy to work with the very best.

I thank my friends Nasir Jones and Kanye West for being so inspirational in their work and helping me articulate emotions that seemed impossible to express. I also appreciate them for letting this fan backstage.

Steve Stoute has been an outstanding friend throughout this process, helping me find my voice and letting me know that the work that I am doing is important.

Thanks to my oldest friend, Joel Clark Jr., for being a great friend for forty-three years and letting me tell the story of how we met.

Chris Schroeder helped me edit the book and maintained a crazy amount of enthusiasm while doing so. Chris blows me away with his interest in this work. Many times, he seems even more interested than I am.

Thank you, Herb Allen, for being a great friend and letting me write about you. I know that is not your favorite thing.

I thank all the partners and employees at Andreessen Horowitz who put up with my grouchiness and increased profanity as I wrote this. It would not have been possible without you. Thank you for making the dream of a firm for founding CEOs come true.

A special thank-you to Margit Wennmachers for believing that I had something to say and helping me find people who would hear it. I am so lucky to be working in the presence of such greatness.

Grace Ellis has been by my side throughout the process, handling every weird detail that one could imagine. During this time, I have yet to hear her complain about a single thing. Beyond that, she has given me great advice and been a great friend.

Thank you, Ken Coleman, for giving me my first job and being a fantastic mentor for nearly thirty years.

Thanks to my brother in-law, Cartheu Jordan Jr., for being an important character in this book and in my life. He is Branch Rickey to my Jackie Robinson.

Thank you, John and Loretta Wiley, for being so supportive of me in everything that I do.

Thanks to my brothers and sisters Jonathan Daniel, Anne Rishon, and Sarah Horowitz for shaping me. Love you always, Sarah.

I thank the late, great Mike Homer for his wisdom, help, and love. I thank Andy Rachleff for being a great gentleman and friend. Thank you, Sy Lorne, for keeping me out of trouble. Thank you, Mike Volpi, for being on the board of a very scary company.

Finally, thank you, Boochie, Red, and Boogie, for being the best children that I could imagine.

# CREDITS

Grateful acknowledgment is made for permission to reproduce from the following:

"Gorgeous," words and music by Malik Jones, Gene Clark, Jim McGuinn, Kanye West, Ernest Wilson, Mike Dean, Scott Mescudi, and Corey Woods. Copyright © 2010 Universal Music Corp.; Jabriel Iz Myne, Tickson Music Co.; Sixteen Stars Music, EMI Blackwood Music, Inc.; Please Gimme My Publishing, Inc.; Papa George Music; Chrysalis Music; Let the Story Begin Publishing; Gene Clark Music; Elsie's Baby Boy; Beautiful Sekai Publishing; and Chrysalis One Songs. All rights for Jabriel Iz Myne controlled and administered by Universal Music Corp. All rights for Sixteen Stars Music controlled and administered by Horipro Entertainment Group, Inc. All rights for Please Gimme My Publishing, Inc., and Papa George Music controlled and administered by EMI Blackwood Music, Inc. All rights for Let the Story Begin Publishing controlled and administered by Chrysalis Music Group, Inc., a BMG Chrysalis Company. All rights for Gene Clark Music controlled and administered by Bug Music, Inc., a BMG Chrysalis Company. All rights for Chrysalis One Songs controlled and administered by BMG Rights Management (Ireland), Ltd. All rights for Elsie's Baby Boy controlled and administered by Kobalt Music Publishing America. All rights for Beautiful Sekai Publishing controlled and administered by Shelly Bay Music. All rights reserved. Used by permission. Reprinted by permission of Hal Leonard Corporation, Kobalt Music Publishing America, Shelly Bay Music, and Alfred Music Publishing.

"Who We Be," words and music by Earl Simmons and Mickey Davis. Copyright © 2001 Boomer X Publishing, Inc.; Dead Game Publishing; Fifty Four Vill Music, LLC; and Kobalt Music Publishing America. All rights for Boomer X Publishing, Inc., controlled and administered by Universal Music Corp. All rights for Dead Game Publishing controlled and administered by EMI April Music, Inc., and Kobalt Music Publishing America. Fifty Four Vill Music, LLC, controlled and administered by the Royalty Network, Inc. All rights reserved. Used by permission. Reprinted by permission of Hal Leonard Corporation, the Royalty Network, Inc., and Kobalt Music Publishing America.

# ABOUT THE AUTHOR

**Ben Horowitz** is the cofounder and general partner of Andreessen Horowitz, a Silicon Valley–based venture capital firm that invests in entrepreneurs building the next generation of leading technology companies. The firm's investments include Airbnb, GitHub, Facebook, Pinterest, and Twitter. Previously he was cofounder and CEO of Opsware, formerly Loudcloud, which was acquired by Hewlett-Packard for $1.6 billion in 2007. Horowitz writes about his experiences and insights from his career as a computer science student, software engineer, cofounder, CEO, and investor in a blog that is read by nearly ten million people. He has also been featured in the *Wall Street Journal*, the *New York Times*, the *New Yorker*, *Fortune*, the *Economist*, and *Bloomberg Businessweek*, among others. Horowitz lives in the San Francisco Bay Area with his wife, Felicia.